'Surprisingly enough, thi
sure, it will help a lot ot p~~r
it quick fixes, magic wands or infuriating "Christian
platitudes. Just personal realism and practical, biblical
wisdom. But that's precisely what you would hope from
a collection of pastors' testimonies! I hope and pray that
it helps pastors feel less isolated and church members
less confused when depression rears its ugly head.'

**Mark Meynell, Director Langham Preaching (Europe &
Caribbean), author *When Darkness Seems My Closest Friend***

'This book invites you into the inner life of pastors who
suffer from depression. It will be an eye-opener to many
people. It will help pastors who suffer similarly to see
that they are not alone and encourage them that God
is still with them. It will also enable church members
to support their pastors more intelligently especially in
prayer. It is an important book for our times.'

**John Benton, Director for Pastoral Support,
The Pastors' Academy, London Seminary**

'This fallen world is full of pain – and our pastors are not immune – but all too often their struggles go unheard. In this raw and honest work, some powerful stories are told. We meet real men who know the depths of depression. And, as we hear from them, we are all better equipped to listen, love and pray with hope for those in ministry. An important work for pastors who are currently struggling alone – and for congregation members who care.'

Helen Thorne, Director of Training and Resources, Biblical Counselling UK

edited by Stephen Kneale

the pastor with a thorn in his side

stories of ministering with
depression and what the
church can do to help

Grace
Publications

Grace Publications

www.gracepublications.co.uk

British Library Cataloguing in Publication Data. A record for this book is available from the British Library

Scripture quotations have been taken from the Christian Standard Bible®, Copyright © 2017 by Holman Bible Publishers. Used by permission. Christian Standard Bible® and CSB® are federally registered trademarks of Holman Bible Publishers.

First published in Great Britain in 2021

Cover design by Pete Barnsley (CreativeHoot.com)

ISBN: 978-1-912154-31-9

Printed in Denmark by Nørhaven

1 3 5 7 9 10 8 6 4 2

Contents

Introduction

Stephen Kneale

If you're reading this book then I'm willing to bet one of three things: one, you are currently suffering from symptoms of depression, two, you have suffered them in the past, or, three, you know of someone who is. Even if none of these things apply to you, then it's reasonable to suggest that they might at some point in the future.

The fact is, mental health issues – particularly those associated with depression and anxiety – are incredibly common. A 2014 NHS research paper found that 1-in-6 people have a common mental health disorder.[1] And according to the mental health charity Mind, 1-in-4 people in England will experience some form of mental health problem each year. The Mental Health Foundation,

1

who have been tracking the effect of the coronavirus pandemic, report that indicators of loneliness, suicidality and an inability to cope with stress are worse now than they were at the start of 2020.[2] Mental health issues are all around us. While it's always hard to quantify these things, it's not a stretch to suggest that we live during a time when these issues are particularly heightened.

Despite the prevalence of mental health issues in society, many Christians still believe that pastors don't really get depressed. Others might struggle in that way, so the sentiment goes, but pastors, surely, are more resilient. At any rate, isn't the church more nurturing and the Holy Spirit doing something or other (it's never quite clear what) so that pastors don't suffer in that way? Others accept that pastors suffer from depression but, as someone once commented to me, 'I didn't think pastors got depressed *like that!*' In other words, its perfectly reasonable for pastors to occasionally feel a bit down, but pastors don't get so ill that they need to be hospitalised or become suicidal.

This book exists to show that pastors, like other Christians, are not immune to the trials and effects of depression and anxiety. It features seven short biographies (including my own) of pastors and church workers who have faced or continue to live with mental health issues that have impacted their lives and their ministry. But, more than that, this book exists to equip and help church members and ministers alike to know how to help those who are struggling in this way. It doesn't argue for prescriptive solutions but by looking at multiple experiences it does suggest that there are helpful or unhelpful ways of approaching mental health issues in pastors.

A recent piece of research conducted by LifeWay found that 23% of pastors said they had personally struggled with some kind of mental health illness.[3] Although these figures come from the church in the US, they mirror the statistics in the wider population in the UK. In short, they tell us that pastors get depression too, even seriously so. Of course, you don't have to look very far in the Christian press to find such stories.

None of this should come as a surprise. We live in a fallen world where the effects of sin and death are all around us. Regardless of money, status, fame or intellect, people get ill and die. As sinful people living in a sinful world, pastors are not exempt. Few deny that church leaders get sick. When a pastor gets cancer or faces a serious operation, most congregants don't automatically assume the pastor is at fault for their illness. We recognise Jesus' teaching that there is no straight line between sin, suffering and illness (John 9:1–3). That doesn't mean sin never leads to illness (cf. John 5:14). The addict who damages themself through ongoing sinful choice or the person with Munchausen's syndrome pretending to be sick and receiving unnecessary and damaging treatment are both cases in point. But the line between sickness and sin – according to Jesus – is not typically a direct or causal one.

Even if there were a tight link between health and holiness (and, for the avoidance of any doubt, there is not), our pastors are no more holy than any other believer. If we are in Christ, we are perfectly holy (cf. 1 Peter 2:9; Ephesians 1:4, 4:24; 1 John 3:3; 1 Corinthians 3:17). No Christian can be any more holy than they already are and none of us are more holy than any other believer. We all have Jesus' perfect righteousness accredited to our account and the Father looks on us through the prism of His Son's perfection (Romans 5:1-5; Ephesians 4:24; Colossians 1:22; 2 Timothy 1:9; 1 Peter 2:9). That means your pastor – as good a man as he may be – is no more holy than you. They sin just like other people but they are also as holy as everyone else who has been made perfectly holy in Christ. They have the same Holy Spirit dwelling in them that every other believer has received too (Romans 8:9, 11; 1 Corinthians 3:16, 6:19; Galatians 4:6; 2 Timothy 1:14). If we recognise that none of these things keep most Christians from suffering the effects of illness, we must accept that pastors will get ill too. Mental health disorders are just one form of illness that has plagued the world since the fall and which affect pastors as much as anybody else.

One pastor who wrote a chapter in this book did not feel able to share his mental health struggles with his church until he read about other ministers who had suffered similar experiences. For some, there is still a stigma associated with mental illness. Others feel a sense of shame and embarrassment. Still others feel they are alone in their experience. This book has been written to assure pastors struggling with depressive illnesses, and churches who recognise that one of their leaders is suffering from a mental health disorder, that they are not alone. These issues are not unique to you. Others suffer with them too and there is no shame in admitting your need for help. Every contributor in this book hopes that this collection of stories makes it clear to both church leaders and their members that depression and anxiety respect no person. Pastors suffer from these things as well and they, as much as anybody else, require the care of their churches in tackling these issues.

Of course, it is one thing to know that others are facing similar situations, it is quite another to know what to do about it. In reality, few experiences of depression are exactly the same. There may be common features, but the circumstances are almost always different. That is the second reason this book has been written. Useful as it may be to read one pastor's experience, the multiple viewpoints presented in this book show the range of ways depression might impact ministry and suggests that each individual situation requires its own particular solution.

This book is not only aimed at pastors struggling with depression. It also exists to help churches care well for those who are suffering from mental health illness in ministry. All of the contributors have included examples of things that were particularly helpful to them as well as things that were especially unhelpful. Many well-meaning folks want to help but just don't know how. It is easy to be paralysed by the fear of getting it wrong and then, ultimately, doing nothing. Others want to help but end up saying or doing something that makes matters worse. This book is for people who want to help, who want to know what to do, but don't know where to start.

But above all of that, this book wants to help you care well for your church leader. It wants to draw out the things that you can do that would be helpful to any pastor suffering with anxiety or depression, as well as identifying the sort of things that are never helpful but somehow seem to keep being done regardless. From these different stories, the conclusion will pull together the common things that helped everyone, the things that didn't help anyone and those things that were different in each case. This will aid those looking to support a church leader suffering with depression to be sensitive in the help they offer.

In the end, we hope this book helps pastors to have honest conversations with their churches about their mental health struggles and we trust, even in some small way, it serves to take away some of the stigma surrounding depression in ministry. We hope those suffering with depressive illnesses might find healing in its pages as they see their situation is not unique and, though it may not feel like it, others really do know something of what it is like. Most of all, we hope it helps churches to support their pastors and church leaders who are struggling in this way. We want it to take away some of the awkwardness of asking for, and offering, help. Likewise, we want this book to highlight the things that are likely to make matters worse and instead encourage us all to aim for what is truly helpful.

Finally, before diving into the stories featured in this book, it's worth outlining a working definition of depression. The NHS helpfully states that 'depression is more than feeling unhappy or fed up for a few days. Most people go through periods of feeling down, but when you're depressed you feel persistently sad for weeks or months.'[4] To receive a formal diagnosis of depression, at least five out of nine symptoms on the DSM-IV classification system must be present for at least two weeks and, during that period, reach 'sufficient severity' for most of every day. The nine symptoms are:

- Persistent sadness or low mood
- Loss of interests and/or pleasure
- Disturbed sleep
- Decreased or increased appetite and/or weight
- Fatigue or loss of energy
- Poor concentration or indecisiveness

- Feelings of worthlessness or excessive or inappropriate feelings of guilt
- Suicidal thoughts or acts[5]

Mild depression is classified as having few, if any, symptoms in excess of the requisite five needed for diagnosis. Sufferers of mild depression often have minor functional impairment. Moderate depression is where symptoms and functional impairment are between mild and severe. Severe depression is where most, if not all, of the symptoms are present and have a significant impact on function. Severe depression may also come with psychotic symptoms.

1

Steve's Story

Stephen Kneale, Pastor,
Oldham Bethel Church

My most serious bout of depression came just after I moved to a new area of the country and took up my first full-time job as a secondary school teacher, hot on the heels of getting married. This was when I was first diagnosed. Up until then, I knew almost nothing about depression but after my diagnosis it became apparent that my depression had been caused years earlier. What is more, with the benefit of hindsight, it was clear that I had already faced other, less significant, depressive episodes before the most serious one.

Early signs

If I was to pinpoint a specific underlying cause, it is probably best described as 'chemical imbalance'. As a child, I had been placed on antidepressants for an issue entirely unrelated to mental health for their helpful side-effects. In my teens, I had a different medical problem (also unrelated to mental health) and was given some medication to address that problem. Those pills, however, are well known to induce depression. It is likely this combination of medicines lay behind my particular illness. Though the groundwork was laid in my childhood, I didn't actually experience any significant bouts of depression until years later.

As a teenager, I strongly suspect I had some minor episodes that led to months of low mood. Nothing, of course, that stopped me functioning. I had parents at home who kept me regimented, meaning there was no opportunity to pull the duvet over my head and stay in bed. There was very little to stress about and so nothing particularly triggering that would cause low mood and lethargy to turn into anything more serious.

By university, I found myself on a course that required little weekly contact time. Again, there was very little to stress about. But it was during my first year that I suffered my first serious bout of depression. It certainly wasn't my worst episode. I didn't go to a doctor and at the time didn't recognise it as depression. But in hindsight, that is exactly what it was.

I remember that, out of the blue, I found myself feeling very low and anxious. I assumed it was the result of being away from home for the first time and figured everybody gets down now and then. I hadn't quite realised that not coming out of your room for weeks on end, except to periodically eat, is less normal. My sleep was very erratic, my appetite waned and there was a period of around eight to twelve weeks where I could not face seeing anybody. I confined myself to my room so I didn't have the anxiety of social interaction. I went to no lectures or seminars and tried not to see anybody at all. The demands of my course and the nature of pastoral care by the university were such that my not being around failed to register with anybody. After two or three months, the whole thing lifted and life went back to normal. I never mentioned it to anybody at the time and, for the remainder of university, didn't think about it again. I was totally untroubled by depression for three years or so after that.

The worst episode triggered

My most serious bout of depression struck the same year my wife and I married, setup home and started new jobs. We ended up living (literally) next door to the church in which I spent my teens. The entire church membership trundled past our front door for every meeting, the pastor lived in a house opposite and our back yard was even overlooked by the headquarters of a mission organisation. This setup ended up exacerbating certain problems later on.

I had taken on a role teaching RE, History and Politics at a secondary school. There were a number of issues in the school that made working life awkward. Among them, the school was spread across sites that were a short drive away from each other. My lessons were split across both sites and I was not given a classroom of my own. I was attempting to navigate three different departments and was not supported well. It wasn't very long before I found myself regularly working into the small hours of the morning trying to complete work and setting off relatively early to get into school. There were also some timetable and building issues that meant lunchtime was cut short and it could be difficult to get time to eat. None of these things were major issues by themselves but this was never going to be sustainable and, given the lack of support, nobody really noticed when I began to struggle.

The pattern of work made the usual symptoms of disruption to sleep and changes to appetite easy to explain away as merely the setup at school. I didn't really notice that I had largely stopped eating at home too, lost a lot of weight and wasn't getting much sleep. I still wasn't convinced there was a problem when I began thinking about swinging my car across lanes of traffic as I was driving into work so that I didn't have to go in and face the day. Fleeting thoughts became increasingly more regular and inescapable. My wife and my parents could see the pattern more clearly and I was soon frog-marched down to a doctor, against my will.

I explained my symptoms to the doctor. I didn't think them very serious and kept apologising for wasting his time. We talked through the lack of sleep and loss of appetite, the lowness of mood and the intrusive thoughts. What I called 'thoughts' was apparently suicidal ideation. What I called 'being a bit low' was depression. What I considered the normal teething troubles of trying to find my feet in a new marriage, job and area were, in fact, much more serious than I realised. I left that appointment with a prescription for antidepressants and a diagnosis of Severe-Chronic Depression.

From bad to worse

You might assume things began to get better from there, but that was only the beginning. I pressed on at work for a while but the medication had no effect. My suicidal ideation grew, leading to a growing desire to do almost anything to avoid the day and actively planning how I could end my life. When I arrived at school, I would be drenched in sweat due to the anxiety of going in, either throwing up or having severe stomach cramps, followed by the inevitable evacuation (let the reader understand), no sooner than I set foot in the school.

After several weeks, I made the mistake of sharing my diagnosis with the head of department charged with my pastoral care. She proceeded to blame me for feeling ill and snarled, 'What on earth does somebody aged twenty-two possibly have to feel depressed about?' She even suggested that it must say something about my wife that depression only kicked in after getting married. I went to a deputy head and resolved to be honest. I didn't get through my first sentence before breaking down in tears. I was swiftly sent home. It was to be the last time I set foot in that school.

I was immediately signed off work by my doctor. My lack of sleep had developed into full-blown insomnia, I developed restless-leg-syndrome and found myself constantly shaking. In one strange episode, I had my first and only psychotic break. I was awake in the middle of the night (as usual) and could clearly hear a crowd of people shouting and jeering outside our house. When I went to look, nobody was there but I could still hear them. By now, I was on two separate antidepressants, a sedative and a sleeping pill. What felt like enough drugs to put down a rhino still only gave me around three or four hours sleep at night.

My depression continued to deepen and suicidal thoughts developed further. I actively investigated how to kill myself. My wife took to hiding medication and sharp objects, daily fearing what she would find when she came home. I attempted to throw myself off a bridge near our home but my wife talked me down. Had I been in my right mind, I would have noticed it was a low bridge over a bit of river that I saw people jumping into a day or two earlier for fun!

In another misguided effort, I decided to try and

bury myself in snow to see if hypothermia would take me. I went home soaked-through feeling very foolish. I didn't realise that a full search party was underway as my wife had come home to find Internet searches on our computer about tying nooses. When she couldn't find me, she drew the obvious conclusion. This made me feel all the more stupid when I returned home. I took to driving as erratically as possible in the hope I might damage myself. I also started to goad local teenagers in the hope one of them might have a knife and take it upon themselves to harm me. But, in our sleepy market town, it served only to traumatise some perfectly decent, unsuspecting kids. All of these choices were utterly foolish. They were neither right nor would they work. But being out of one's mind leads, unsurprisingly, to some colossally poor decision-making.

Seeking further help

Eventually, my wife contacted a local crisis team for support. They would not help beyond asking me to ring them if I felt suicidal. I explained that if I was suicidal, I was unlikely to call because they would try to stop me. Apparently that answer did not compute and they said there was nothing more they could do. Finally, after one of the failed attempts on my life, I was referred to a local hospital. I was not keen to go but was told, if I refused, they would section me. I wasn't so stupid as to want that, so I complied.

I was immediately thrown into group therapy. In the first session, I endured person after person relaying how their depression stemmed from their time at school and the teachers who treated them badly. As a teacher, it was not a very helpful environment and I felt incredibly guilty, taking each story personally despite having nothing to do with any of them. I was told I had to go to the hospital every day for six weeks, which I duly did. The agreement was that if I went to the hospital each day, I would be allowed home in the evenings. By the end of six weeks, I was assured I was much better. I did not feel any better.

By this time, I had been placed under the care of a psychiatric consultant. She reviewed my medication and prescribed some pills that lifted my mood in a way that nothing had worked before. I began to feel well enough to engage more helpfully with talking therapies. My church – who at this point had been made aware of what was going on and were praying for me – offered to pay for some private counselling. The counselling did not make me better, but I remember it being broadly helpful at the time.

Having been signed off from work for quite a while longer, I had a visit from the headteacher asking if I intended to come back to school. I was in no fit state to work and, in the end, my employment was terminated. Nevertheless, by the end of that year, I experienced enough uplift in my mood that I was not continually suicidal and was able to function to a certain degree. My wife's job, which was fixed to a year's contract, ended and, just as things started to lift for me, we had to move to a different area of the country.

The beginning of the end

Three things at that time were God's specific provision for us. First, I was well enough that I needed something to do but was not yet able to get back into full-time work. I had wanted to undertake further study at some point in the future; the doctor suggested this might be helpful in the immediate term to offer some focus. I looked into theological courses but decided I would need to do it flexibly so that if I had bad days it wouldn't be a problem. I looked into various colleges and found one that offered an online distance-learning course. My fees were generously paid for by others who recognised the course would help me. Not only did it give me some focus as I reached a point of recovery, but unknown to me, the Lord would later use this as His means of moving me into ministry (I had no designs on ministry at the time).

We attended a small, quiet church where we had moved. There was very limited gospel outreach going on. This was the Lord's second special provision for us. With little outreach going on, there was very little pressure to serve. This was so significant as I would have largely been unable to do it. I would also have inevitably felt guilty for not doing it, despite being in no fit state to serve in that way at that time.

Most amazingly, totally unknown to us when we joined, one of the elders of that church happened to be a consultant psychiatrist. He agreed to see me privately in his own time. Up to then, I had found the Cognitive Behavioural Therapy I received to be wholly ineffective. The statements of fact against which they asked me to judge my feelings were so open to interpretation that they never helped. But this elder did two important things. First, he explained that CBT may not make me feel any better, but it would help me think and act better. Before this, I often felt personal blame for CBT not working but his comment took all the pressure of it away. As soon as I could see what it was designed to do, it began to achieve what I was told it should. The second thing he did was to point me to what the Bible said about me. He knew I was a Christian and said, 'You wouldn't argue with the Bible, would you?' We both knew that was true. When we looked into the Scriptures and saw, not what I felt about myself, but what the Lord thought about me, who was I to argue? The statements of fact that, as far as I was concerned were not open to interpretation, had been found. This had such a significant impact on me and was vital in my recovery.

We soon had to move again. The depression was still there, but I was now able to function more fully and look at getting back into work. I spent a year or so searching for work but eventually grew tired and decided to work for myself. Having completed my MA by distance-learning, I was well used to self-directing my work from home. We got stuck into a local church and, some time during that next year, that most serious episode of depression finally came to an end. It had gone on for two-and-a-half years.

Since then, I have remained on antidepressants. I once attempted to come off, which did not end well, and I promptly went back on them again. It is likely I will be on them in perpetuity. Most of the time, I am perfectly fine, functioning normally and happily without depression. But I still face what are best described as periodic dips. Nothing nearly as serious as what has been described here, but nonetheless bouts of low mood, the inability to concentrate and difficulties sleeping and eating. I have, since that worst episode, not been so ill that I had to stop work but depression still rears its head from time to time. I find that it is always there, lurking in the background, even if it is somewhat more muted these days.

Well-meaning but unhelpful

I have already described our living setup when my depression was at its worst. Whilst this is nobody's fault, the reality of feeling as though we were living in a goldfish bowl had a serious impact on my anxiety. I used to get panic attacks at the thought of opening the door and hearing folks we knew walking past. The mission building behind our back wall was such that it felt they could see right into our home and made me think that they were watching us at all times. Of course, they weren't but when anxiety levels are through the roof, and paranoia is running rampant, all of this adds to the intensity of the situation.

The pastor living across the road from us added another layer of complication. Not only did it fuel the feeling of constantly being watched (which was not his fault) but he had a habit of running out of his house any time he saw me to see how I was doing. I appreciate he wanted to ensure I was okay but, in reality, it caused me great anxiety – as most social interaction did – and I would find myself creeping out so I could avoid him. I would open the door, looking this way and that to check that the coast was clear. One time, when he clocked me through his window, I had made it to my car and thought myself safe. But as I was driving off, he leapt in front of the bonnet so I had to talk to him. Little did he know I was seriously contemplating running him down so I didn't have to endure the anxiety of speaking to him! If you are looking to help somebody who is depressed, this sort of thing is best avoided.

A number of folks came to visit. I will explain how some people helped, but there were a number of ways others didn't. Constantly being asked, 'What can we do to help?' was probably the most common unhelpful thing. Along with my depression came significant feelings of guilt. This question always heaped more guilt on top. Most people, of course, genuinely do want to help and are asking how best to do so. Unfortunately, when you are depressed and so full of guilt that you can't achieve anything, it creates another task for you to do. Not only was I in no fit state to undertake it, but I also felt guilty that I couldn't find things for people to do that might be helpful.

Similarly, I found visitors staying for long periods of time difficult to manage. I was largely unable to concentrate on anything. I certainly wasn't able to read and, when I tried praying, I would forget my thoughts almost as soon as they came. When people decided to stay for an hour, it was just too long. I couldn't keep up with the conversation and the mental energy involved in preparing for the visit and trying to engage with it was exhausting. Shorter visits were almost always better.

Others decided to ask me how I was doing. That was always unhelpful because it usually felt like they were saying, 'Are you still ill? Surely you must be feeling a bit better by now?' Again, it induced a lot of guilt when the answer was 'No,' or 'Actually, I'm feeling worse.' Given the high levels of guilt at which I was operating, being asked how I was tended to feel more like an accusation. It is far better to let the person tell you how they are doing – should they want to share that – rather than probe into whether they have experienced any lift yet. These sorts of questions can give the impression that we have compassion fatigue and wish this person would just pull themselves together.

It was not uncommon to have people tell me that they knew how I felt too. Sometimes, bizarrely, having just asked me how I felt! They would then relay their story of having suffered depression which, from where I was sitting, was nothing like mine. One person whose story did have similarities to mine – and it really wasn't identical but the effects were just as serious – was one of a few people who insisted he didn't know what I was feeling. Those who insist they know how you feel are invariably the ones with the least insight. We would do well to avoid that assumption and just let the other person tell you instead.

It seems important to say here that not all the medication and talking therapies were helpful. I am not saying this to put anybody off taking theirs – if you have been prescribed medication, take it! I mention it so that we are realistic about what to expect. I am currently on pills that are very effective for me and I did receive some particularly helpful counselling once it was sorted out. But to get to that point, I took various medicines that achieved very little and some of the talking therapies I was given were of no help at all. It took a long time to discover what was effective. The key was to press on until I found the things that worked.

Help in the depths

Without doubt, the most helpful thing was finding the right medication. I am convinced that, without it, nothing else would have worked for me. The pills brought me to a point where I could engage with other therapies. For a long time, those therapies just did not work because the right medicine had not been found and I was too unwell to benefit from them. Though certain pills did nothing, and others made me worse, finding the right ones in the end made the biggest difference to me. Those same pills are what, even now, keep my depression largely at bay.

Whilst I initially found CBT useless, when it was delivered more helpfully it did begin to make some difference. Perversely, perhaps, what made it useful was knowing that it might not help. That took the pressure off. Also, it works by finding objective statements of fact that cannot be argued against. As Christians, we would do well to root those statements in Scripture because most of us aren't going to argue with them!

In smaller ways, a number of people were helpful. When I couldn't see people due to anxiety, I appreciated everybody who posted short notes to say they were praying for me. I couldn't concentrate to read much, but a short note to assure me of prayer was always well received. Similarly, some people left little gifts outside my door to say they were thinking of me too. They wanted to show that they cared without causing me more anxiety. I found that thoughtfulness really helpful.

One time, a friend of ours who owns a farm took me out to pick elderflowers so we could make some cordial. He wasn't a big talker which was a boon. He simply drove me to his farm, picked some flowers and then quietly went back to his house and made cordial. It was helpful because it got me outside doing a bit of exercise, didn't require lots of talking and wasn't mentally exerting. It also filled up an entire afternoon and, at the end of it, had some product giving a sense of achievement. This helped me enormously. I appreciate not everybody has access to a farm, but quietly taking somebody with you to do something lightly physical, that doesn't require any talking, can help. If it is something that gives a sense of achievement, no matter how small, that is better. I found building flatpack furniture was similarly helpful.

Lastly, the passage of time proved helpful. When you feel so very low, to the point of suicide, you are desperate for relief. But depression is normally a long time coming and you can't expect something that has been months or years in the making to disappear overnight. If I had known for sure that everything would have lifted within eighteen months, I might have been less inclined to attempt to take my life. Though we don't know when, the chances are that things will eventually lift. Knowing this from the start can be a real help when we just want to give up. Reminding people of this fact does no harm.

How to keep going

In ministry, I have built things into my work to manage the fact that I might get ill. First, continuing to take my medication is key. I am able to function well on them so must consistently take my pills. When I do face dips, being on the medication means that they will only ever get so bad.

I have also set myself up so that I prepare sermons with a significant buffer of time, usually about three or four months ahead of when they are due to be delivered. This gives me wiggle room if I am experiencing a dip and I am finding work difficult to manage. If I miss a week of sermon preparation, it doesn't matter as far as the upcoming Sunday is concerned. I can always make up the shortfall when I am feeling more able. I have to pace myself when it comes to visitation and evangelistic work in similar ways.

I also continue to be open with my elders. When I am experiencing downturns, I try to tell them as soon as I can. Whilst I haven't yet had an episode so serious that I lose all function, the dips necessarily affect what I can do. Having good, supportive elders in place who are able to pick up any potential slack from my downturns has been a real blessing. Thankfully, I haven't yet failed to do something I was supposed to do because of depression, but it does remain a live possibility. Being open with my church – and particularly with the elders who serve alongside me – has been important.

2

Dave's Story

Dave Williams, Former Pastor,
Bearwood Chapel, Smethwick

When it hit

Things started for me after a busy Sunday morning at the end of a hectic week in November 2019. I had already preached twice, tried to resolve various technical hitches and followed that up with a difficult pastoral conversation. Suddenly, I found myself sitting in the church lounge sobbing and thinking, 'I just can't go on anymore.' Following a conversation with another elder (who just happened to be an NHS consultant) we agreed that I needed to take some time out. I started by 'benching' myself from leading and speaking at a baptism service that was due to take place that evening.

The next day, I went to see my doctor. I initially

picked up a ticket to see a locum, but it turned out they weren't in work that day and I ended up seeing one of the practice GPs who I knew relatively well. This was a real provision from the Lord.

'What's the problem?' she asked.

I burst into tears and found myself unable to speak.

'This ...' was all I managed to utter.

A little bit later, I was able to say more and tell her that one of our church leaders suggested I might be suffering from burnout. We went through some questions and I was diagnosed with Mixed Anxiety and Depression. I was signed off work for two weeks (this was extended later on) and prescribed the antidepressant Sertraline. I tried, though not wholeheartedly, to negotiate some wriggle room so that I could carry on with some responsibilities (including an upcoming funeral) but the doctor was firm. I was to be signed off from everything.

She said to me plainly, 'I know you. You are not your usual self and not in a good way. I know you want to look after others, but who looks after you? If they don't care for you, you won't be able to help others.'

So it was, I ended up with three weeks on the sofa. My brain seemed to have stopped working to the point where I was unable to even read. I could only manage to string a few sentences together without long pauses. More often than not, all I wanted to do was sleep and maybe stick something mindless on the telly.

The aftermath

I spent about three weeks unable to really think, process or engage with anything much at all. After the initial emotional outpouring, I felt exhausted, like I had been hit hard. Then gradually, I started to rebuild. I went out for short walks and attended church for a service – but made sure I went straight home again afterwards without speaking to too many people.

In the New Year, I found that I could engage more helpfully with things. I was keen to resume preaching, but I wanted to pace myself. I began to get involved again with some pastoral matters and joined in bits of leadership. This mainly meant written correspondence and some short pastoral conversations, either one-to-one or in very small groups.

What I noticed most clearly at this time was that my resilience felt like it had been completely stripped away. Prior to depression hitting me, if a situation proved to be challenging or confrontational (and while I realise that few people enjoy such meetings) I found I would normally bounce back from them quickly enough. Over the years, I've found that a good remedy for the frustrations of church life is getting out: going into the street or knocking on a few doors to share the good news of Jesus. But now, I started to find that I needed more time to prepare for upcoming difficult discussions and, after those meetings, an increasing amount of time to recover.

Perhaps the hardest thing to come back to was our Sunday Night Church. We'd started this meeting back in 2012. It began life as a Bible study over pizza for teens and twenties but had grown into a café-style service. The presence of food had drawn in quite a few rough sleepers and hostel dwellers. They came to eat but increasingly stayed to take part in the service, joining in with the songs, listening to the talks and taking part in the discussion. So, this was a precious and important meeting for me. I had put a lot of work into making it happen and much time into getting to know the people who came along. We were beginning to see signs of gospel fruit. However, the style and structure of the meeting, as well as the variety of chaotic needs of the people involved, suddenly meant that this environment felt unpredictable, uncontrollable and very unsafe to me.

On top of all this, just as I was beginning to feel able to do more, lockdown struck. I'm still not sure what to make of it. On the one hand, I felt like I had already lost a few months and now I was going to be losing even more. On the other, I can fully see God's providence in it all. The best way to explain this is to look at a typical conversation I've had with quite a few people throughout the pandemic. Often, they would say something like: 'Lockdown must be providing you with time to rest and recover.' But they could not have been further from the truth. I didn't need the lockdown after depression. If anything, my illness prepared me for it because it had already taken me through a period of seclusion. Whilst others suddenly had to get used to the isolation of being restricted to home and having their normal routines disrupted, I had already been living that life back in November and December.

Furthermore, if we had gone into lockdown a few months earlier I would have been physically and emotionally unready. My batteries were drained and I was run down. The statements about lockdown helping me recover suggested that it was a peaceful time of rest. Many have described it as a kind of Sabbath. I'm sure it became like that over time for some congregations and pastors. The disruption to normal service allowed us to reflect on what we were doing and why we do it. But the beginning of that pandemic was extra busy. We could not use the normal means to gather God's people, the usual programmes that enabled connection weren't there and so we had to work hard and think creatively. I doubt I would have had the energy and emotional resilience to cope with a week filled with one-to-one walks, consecutive phone calls, Zoom meetings and video talks had this all happened earlier. As it was, I could go into the lockdown at pace and I was able to fill my days. It was later in the year that I again found myself needing time to rest and recover.

In the autumn, and in consultation with my GP, I began to wean myself off my antidepressants. This happened at a less than ideal time. Financial pressures at church meant that my role was coming to an end in December and I was aware of the potential this would have for a severe knockback. This is something that I don't want to underplay. The uncertainty of what might (or, might not) be coming next has the potential to cause great anxiety. What is more, there was a sense of grief, sadness and regret because we were leaving people who we loved and were spiritually growing behind.

However, I have also been aware of God's providential care for me. We spent much of that year looking at the Psalms and their powerful descriptions of life in the valley. It was a year filled with songs that speak about God's goodness and faithfulness. Throughout that time, both the Word and worship constantly reminded me to cling to Christ, to trust in God's goodness and to keep looking forward in hope.

Lead up and warning signs

I started this story on the day that my symptoms of depression and anxiety became apparent. And when depression first hits, that is often how it feels: like it has come out of nowhere. But when you look back, with the benefit of hindsight, you realise that the warning signs were always there. Things did not come out of nowhere at all, but were staring you in the face and you missed them. That was certainly true in my case.

In the summer of 2018, I had taken a sabbatical. The plan was to spend a few months on study leave to read, think and write about urban mission. I managed to do a significant proportion of that work but I had underestimated just how emotionally exhausted I was. We saw some core people leave the church and had some bruising pastoral encounters that hit me much harder than I had realised.

Of course, we were busy – as most churches are – and was often told that we 'punched above our weight' in terms of ministry. At that point in time, we ran five weekend congregations to make maximum use of our small building. On a personal level, that wasn't a major issue for me as we had a reasonable preaching team, which meant that I did not have to lead or preach at every service. As you can imagine, there were weekends when bad rota management on my part meant I was speaking at all of the services, but I became better at avoiding those kinds of situations. In any case, I enjoy teaching God's Word and am more likely to feel energised by multiple opportunities to preach. To me, it doesn't feel very different to my wife spending five periods in the classroom, one after the other, as a teacher.

However, I increasingly found myself in charge of the logistics. It was never a case of turning up, talking to a few people, preaching, offering counsel in light of the message then going home. I was there early, making sure everything was set up, discovering the mess and problems left behind by the previous event and addressing the potential issues coming up. Unsurprisingly, this, of course, was the cause of a lot of stress.

The main warning sign that depression was coming was my loss of desire to do things that I would normally relish and enjoy. I was reading a lot less and ruminating on things much more. I usually enjoy the excitement of problem solving and exploring new ideas and ventures but when 2020 arrived, and a host of challenges reared their head, instead of being energised by the opportunity, I was filled with dread.

For example, we were presented with the possibility of acquiring some land next to the church building to enable future development. We had opened a community café a few years earlier but the lead volunteer had decided to stand down so we were going to review how to take the ministry forward. In addition, I had been invited to take a leading role on a steering group looking at the future of our church network. On top of this, there were a number of things happening in terms of church planting and revitalisation that, under other circumstances, would have been very exciting to me. As it was, instead of acting as a catalyst and driving these things forward, I felt like I was desperately trying to put my foot on the break to slow us down.

In the summer of 2020, the Covid-19 lockdown restrictions were eased. We were able to travel and see a few people before going on holiday. During one excursion, my wife suddenly said, 'You're back!' We had been talking all the way on the journey. She then shared with me that she had been growing concerned because I often seemed to shut down. In the car, I would spend a whole journey in silence. This wasn't like me at all. She had also observed that our holiday the previous year hadn't done its usual magic. I had not seemed to unwind and there didn't seem to be any rest, refreshment or renewal.

Helps and hindrances

Given that my brush with depression is fairly recent, I am still learning how to live with its aftereffects. Moreover, the timing of when my illness struck – in the midst of a global pandemic – meant I have been recovering without access to a number of things that would ordinarily be available. For example, I talked with my GP about the possibility of counselling early on, but this became a low priority as the health service was forced to deal with more pressing matters. In the absence of formal counselling, I had to rely on a certain amount of self-talk. It has been helpful to have wells of experience to draw from: past experiences of counselling, books I had read, seminars I had attended. I may not have had a counsellor to talk to in real time but past learning and experience has provided the counsellor's voice to question, challenge and advise. I by no means want to underplay the value of counselling for pastors strug- gling with mental health issues; it is simply to say that counselling was not readily available in my case.

In truth, our church family were largely loving and caring without prying. I felt it right to share my diagno- sis with the church early on. That is not always possible for everyone, but it was the right thing in our situation. It was lovely to get visits and calls from church members who came to sit and chat. It was a great encouragement to see that younger members were maturing in com- passion and care. There were so many helpful things. Some surprising. This included the thoughtfulness and prayers of others. I found comfort in the Psalms and in listening to some beautiful hymns and songs, especially those that talk about God's faithful care, His goodness and His love.

However, not everything that was done was helpful. In one instance, I picked up on the grape vine that people were engaging in speculation about my illness. It seemed one rumour going around was that I was suffering from something much more serious, and certainly different, to what I had told the church. At the same time, conversely, I found out that another rumour led to my diagnosis being questioned altogether. This was both unhelpful and dangerous. I do not know why some presume to know better than a qualified doctor and even more so when they haven't seen the person in question themselves. Those suggesting that I had faked my illness fail to contend with the fact that it is highly unlikely a pastor – or many men – would say they were depressed unless this was truly the case. There is still a strong body of opinion within evangelicalism that sees depression as a sign of weakness or a sign of deeper spiritual problems. Some want to insist that the depressed pastor is a failed pastor. On top of that, when others rely on you, when you get sick and have to stop, it is easy to see why you might feel like you have failed them and let them down.

Alongside that, I received some very prescriptive advice from a couple of people who decided that my experience was exactly the same as their own. As such, they were sure that I should approach my recovery in the same way as them. I am sure they meant well but it was ultimately quite unhelpful. In some circumstances, that advice also came with a dose of legalism. Once again, the undertone was that this illness was a failure on my part.

Honey from the rock

Over the past couple of years, it has been a privilege to teach through the book of Deuteronomy. I love the imagery of the words in Deuteronomy 32:13, 'He nourished him with honey from the rock'.

There is something about the hard toil of a tough hike in the blazing sun that means, when we do stop for food and drink, it is so much more refreshing. God provided water from a rock in the wilderness, but there was something especially refreshing and sweet about it. Honey from the rock. Similarly, I love the first prayer in *The Valley of Vision* which talks about the valley and the depths being the place where we see God's vision and gaze at the stars. These words hold a special place in my heart since finding myself in the depths. It has been in the darkness, in the depths of a deep valley, dry and thirsty, that I have discovered anew God's kindness and tenderness to me. There has been sweetness like honey as I've learnt to cling on to Christ.

3

Alistair's Story

Alistair Chalmers, Assistant Pastor, Bruntsfield Evangelical Church, Edinburgh

Have you ever wandered into church and felt sick at what you were seeing? 120 smiling, happy faces. 120 people seemingly living a hassle-free life, which you know you are not. You seem to be looking at 120 Christians whose lives are not that different from the social media page that they regularly update. Their Instagram life seems to match their Christian life. But the reality is that a lot of people turn up on a Sunday wearing a mask, pretending they are okay, when they are not. Too often, Christians don't talk about their poor mental health because they feel, as their faith is in Jesus, they should always be happy – or at least pretend to be. This results in people feeling isolated and struggling in silence, thinking that they are the only ones who are in a battle. Not only is this incorrect, but it creates a culture where people hide their true selves. That was my story.

My journey with depression started a long time before I became a pastor. My experience is likely to be similar to the experience of a church member with depression and it has shaped how I approach ministry today. As difficult as my depression was, I do believe that it has made me a better pastor, someone who can sympathise with members who feel the same. Depression is a difficult illness that can rob people of joy, steal any sense of emotion and almost drown a person in sorrow and emptiness. There are so many people in pews and pulpits who suffer from depression. The church needs to actively create a culture where people, both member and minister, can openly discuss their vulnerabilities and find help.

Where it all began

I was born and raised in a Christian home in North Wales to Scottish parents. I grew up in the church and heard the Bible being taught. My father was an elder in the church and he preached regularly and my mother was a very active member. I was also home-schooled, along with other families from the same church, using an American Christian system. There was nothing wrong with my childhood, no triggers or traumas that would lead to my depression. When I was twelve my family and I uprooted to Romania where my parents became missionaries. This move is something that we had been anticipating for a long time and talked about for years as a family. I was really looking forward to it. I liked the idea of living in a new country, learning a new language, making new friends and experiencing a different culture. I had no idea how different my life would be in just a few years. I had grown up in a bit of a Christian bubble and then I was moving to a completely new country, a new world. It would turn out to be something of a rollercoaster, but those details are beyond this chapter's scope.

Initially my family and I moved to Romania to work with the large homeless population but eventually moved to a small village where my parents pastored a church. I say all of this because on the outside, everything seemed fine. Onlookers could see that I was raised by Christians, lived on the mission field and was even translating my father's sermons for him week in and week out. Surely the way I was acting meant that I was okay, but it was not the case.

The beginnings of the storm

From an early age I had learned what people around me, specifically Christians, wanted to hear. I had learned what they wanted to see a young 'Christian boy' doing. I was happy to please people and meet their expectations, so I played along. I had the Sunday mask that I wore whenever I was around Christians. I would always have a smile on and looked the part. I used the language that I knew people wanted to hear and the words that they would praise. Nobody taught me to do this or expected me to be someone I wasn't. Yet, for some reason, I felt the need to pretend that I was a Christian. I knew the gospel, I even said I believed it and was baptised, but I was living my life under false pretenses. I was trying to live in my own strength. Reflecting on my earlier years now, I realise that the mask I wore was probably an image of the person I wanted to be. I wanted to be the Christian kid that believed the gospel, but instead of opening up about it I took a fake-it-till-you-make-it approach. For a while I got away with it and no one was aware that anything was wrong.

At around the age of fifteen, something changed. I can't pinpoint one particular cause to my depression. A relationship I was in ended. The youth group I was in became a bit uncomfortable. I was a teenage boy. Who knows what the cause was? Regardless, I began to have dark thoughts. I began to feel lonely even though our house was often busy with teams from different countries coming to help my parents with their work. I could be in a house full of people yet feel completely alone. I began to doubt everything; to question whether anything I knew or felt was even real. My mind would spin as if I were on a roundabout with no exit. Instead of talking to people about this and trying to get the help that I now know I needed, I continued to wear my mask and threw myself into a new job working on a small farm. During the hours of hard work and physical labour, I didn't have to think about my life or whether it had any meaning or not. This was a welcome distraction that kept me from spiralling during the day. It initially kept the dark thoughts at bay.

The storm begins to rage

As time went on, my thoughts began to descend further into hopelessness. I didn't speak to anyone but kept my feelings to myself. I didn't reach out for the help I knew I needed, instead listening to the lies whispering in my mind that I meant nothing. I believed the lie that my friends and family would be better off without me. My first suicidal thoughts began. I started to plan my death and created a fake world in my mind where life without me in it was better and easier for everyone who knew me. Before I knew it, I already had the things that I needed. I had the means, I thought I had the reason, but I couldn't see that it was all a big lie.

For a number of years, I self-harmed almost daily in an attempt to feel something. My depression left a sense of emptiness. I was more of a shell than a person; a shadow of myself. Hurting myself was not out of a desire to do so, but more because I wanted to feel something. I thought it would help, but it only made it worse. I made three attempts to take my own life, each night covering my tracks so that no one knew of my pain or my struggles. All the while, I was actively serving in the church and translating sermons for my father. No one had an inkling of what was going on.

The words I would use to describe my depression are: empty, hollow, dark, grim and despair. There seemed to be no hope. There was no joy. Even slight moments of happiness would be overcast with the dark clouds of depression that followed me day and night. Whilst everyone slept, and the physical darkness came, my thoughts descended into deeper despair. These dark thoughts were fueled by my silence. I now know that if I would have spoken to my parents, and to others around me, help would have been given. I wish I would have taken off my mask. If this is you, I urge you, take off your mask.

Depression can look different for different people. My depression didn't cause any physical limitations, while others struggle to get out of bed. Those around me had no idea what was going on. One of the hardest things was revealing my secret life to my parents several years later. I made sure that there was no way they could have known before then. They were utterly shocked. I had managed to live under the same roof as them for years but hide what I truly felt. I am writing this because depression often isn't visible. There will be those in your congregation, or maybe this is you as a pastor, who will function perfectly well but are broken and crumbling on the inside. Silence does not help. Take off your mask.

Sunshine through the clouds

One night, on my final attempt to take my own life, I was reminded of a verse that had been my favourite since childhood. In John 15:5, Jesus says, 'I am the vine; you are the branches. The one who remains in me and I in him produces much fruit, because you can do nothing without me.' I realised that throughout my entire life I had been trying to do things in my own strength. I was doing everything apart from Jesus and I had come to the end of myself. I realised that I needed to live in Jesus, to confess my weakness and rely on Him. It was a wonderful sensation. It was wonderful because it was freeing. I was no longer constantly trying to be someone else, or pretending to be fine, but I was trusting in the strength of the Almighty God to sustain me. Relying on God's strength, and not my own, meant that I could let go of the foolish idea that I had to do everything by myself, that I was by myself. Confessing my weakness felt good. It was a relief.

My depression didn't stop immediately though. There were many times later on where dark thoughts and the clouds of depression seemed to loom again. However, by God's grace, they have stayed at bay. I no longer have depression and for that I am thankful. Since reflecting and learning more about it, I realise that my healing was unusual, and that won't happen for everyone. My journey didn't involve medication, counselling or external support, which normally help people through their depression (tools that I recommend to everyone who has depression!). I don't know how long it took for the stormy clouds of my depression to disappear; all I know is that things got better over a period of time. God had literally torn me out of my darkest moment. This was an undeserved and unexpected gift. But sadly, there are people who are never freed from the black dog that plagues them (and quoting a Bible verse at them and hoping for healing won't help).

The wave that threw me

When people learn of my history with depression, I am often asked if I would go back and change it all if I could. My initial response is: that's the wrong question to ask. I cannot change my past nor undo what has already happened. God is faithful and He makes no mistakes. But I can look back and be thankful that by God's grace, He carried me through. Charles Spurgeon, who suffered from depression for many years, is often attributed as the one who said, 'I have learned to kiss the wave that throws me against the Rock of Ages.' My depression was the wave that threw me off my own feet and hurled me into the arms of an Almighty God and Wonderful Saviour. For that I will always be thankful. Though the storm raged, tossing me to and fro, I ultimately landed in the safest place I could: the arms of a faithful God.

It was hard to feel the internal anguish that I did. I don't like seeing the scars that are remnants of darker days or having memories of attempted suicides. Looking back on those years certainly isn't an easy exercise that I enjoy. But as hard as those years were – and they were heart-wrenchingly difficult – they eventually brought me to the end of myself and made me run instead to God. Whilst I was in the middle of my depression, I couldn't see what was happening nor understand why it was happening. I'm not sure I even fully grasp it yet, but I know that my experience has helped me help others. The Lord has shown me that in the midst of suffering the question to ask is not, 'Why?' but, 'Who?' Instead of doubting God and running from Him, I learned, as Spurgeon said, to embrace the hardship that threw me into the arms of God.

What now?

Through God's help, I have not experienced depression now for many years and have not endured it whilst in ministry. Yet depression is my constant companion as I walk alongside many whose life is marked, scarred, wounded and sometimes ended by this illness. Maybe you share my story. Maybe you are in the middle of the storm. Perhaps you feel burdened by other's experiences or you are keen to use your own experience with depression to help others.

The church and its pastors have a role to play in caring for the burdened, building others up in the Lord and spurring them on in their Christian walk. All Christtians are called to this work as Ephesians 4:15–16 says:

> But speaking the truth in love, let us grow in every way into him who is the head—Christ. From him the whole body, fitted and knit together by every supporting ligament, promotes the growth of the body for building itself up in love by the proper working of each individual part.

What we say

Regrettably, the way some Christians, including pastors, talk about mental health and depression can be less than helpful. Frankly, I understand why! What can you say to someone like me, who felt no joy in anything? It's easy to feel overwhelmed and out of your depth. We quickly grab our Bibles, quote Psalm 32:11 and say, 'Rejoice in the Lord! All you need to do is turn to Jesus and you'll be fine!' Unfortunately, this often leaves the depressed person feeling worse. It puts the cause of depression on the person's faith. It makes them think, 'Something must be wrong with me and my faith that I just can't be happy in Christ.' Some, just like me, would rather put a mask on every Sunday than have others think of them as a 'bad Christian'.

Nevertheless, the depressed can certainly find comfort in Scripture, and they should! The Bible gives us the biblical language that we can use to express our pain and come before the Lord with our raw emotions, or lack thereof (for example Psalm 77 and 88). Nowhere in the Bible are we promised that if we turn to Jesus all of our troubles will disappear. Whilst not many Christians would explicitly hold to that way of thinking, many can speak in a 'come to Jesus to get fixed and all your problems will disappear' kind of way. This leads to a culture where people feel they need to wear a mask if they are not perfect. The depressed person certainly can be helped through Jesus, He alone is our source of true hope. However, there is no promise in Scripture that if we come to the Lord all of our problems will disappear overnight. Jesus promises to be with His people through thick and thin and to never desert us. As hard as it may sound, Christian hope isn't found in being free of depression either. Our hope is found in the gospel of Jesus Christ, in the promise of an eternity spent in the presence of God and the knowledge that He will never abandon us. That is all true, no matter how hard the storm rages. Walking alongside people with depression can be a long and hard journey. But it is a beautiful journey as you encourage others with Scripture, speak truth in love, help practically and pray patiently.

What we wear

As pastors and church leaders we can, and should, address this issue by being vulnerable. We should be leading examples of what it means to remove the Sunday mask and live openly and honestly in front of the people the Lord has entrusted to us. Some of the most fruitful conversations I've had with Christians were those in which I've opened up about my past and my depression. Not to show how well I'm doing, but recognising that I'm a fallen human being who wants to point others to Jesus. Over the years I have been in one-to-one Bible studies with guys who have depression and it has been a joy to be able to share experiences with them, sympathise with them and help them feel understood. Pastors, we must lead by example and take off our masks and show people the reality that nobody is perfect and that everyone has their own struggles. Our goal should always be to point people to Jesus, to encourage our churches to find their confidence in the gospel and to live out their faith according to the Bible every single day. We can help people feel able and comfortable to talk about their struggles when we, as pastors and leaders (and indeed all Christians), take off our own masks and show vulnerability.

What tools we use

As pastors and leaders, we do not help people in isolation. There are plenty of resources at our disposal, both inside the church and out. I am no medical professional, and I make that clear in every conversation I have about depression. I have not been trained to treat depression. Therefore, it is not my place to diagnose or discuss treatment plans with someone. My goal as a pastor is to care for the depressed soul and help them see hope in the midst of the storm.

Christians, including pastors, need to know that depression isn't necessarily a solely physical or completely spiritual thing. Plenty of helpful research has been conducted over the years which explores the physical reasons for depression and there have also been good resources published on depression from a Christian perspective. However, as I've spoken with Christians over the years, there seems to be an idea that depression, for the Christian, is merely a spiritual issue. If we say that depression is primarily spiritual, then we can find ourselves belittling people's experiences and stop them from seeking the medical help that they might well need. Seeking professional help is not a sign of weakness; I wish I had done that when I was in the midst of my depression.

At the other extreme, depression can also be viewed as purely a medical matter. If we say depression is only physical, then we might stop people thinking through the possibility that there is a spiritual element to their depression. To focus on either extreme runs the risk of us not helping the person and preventing them getting the help they need. Depression is a horrible thing that plagues so many people. The words we use to encourage and challenge the depressed person are important. Ultimately, we might never know why a person has depression. Realistically, we do not need to know. Our job is to help, to pastor and to teach them in their depression and point them to Jesus.

As I continue my journey in the Christian faith, as you journey along your path of depression, or help someone who is depressed, remember the glorious truth that you are never alone. You may not understand why everything is happening to you, you may never know, but the reality is that we don't need to know. We can rest in the knowledge that we have a Saviour who knows our pain, sees our struggles, who cares for and loves us. Every struggle and heartache is a reminder that we live in a sinful, broken world but it is also an opportunity to run into the arms of a loving Saviour.

4

Adam's Story

Adam Thomas, Pastor,
Litchard Mission Church, Bridgend

When I began my first pastorate at Litchard Mission in July 2017, I had been theologically prepared for a lot of challenges, but experiencing depression wasn't one of them. The first year of ministry was filled with encouragements. We were warmly welcomed, there was a wonderful unity in the fellowship, we celebrated the birth of our second child, and much more. Then, completely unexpectedly, just before my one-year pastoring anniversary, I ended up in hospital for thirty-two days. So began my journey with depression.

Where it all began

When I first arrived in A&E, I had spent a few days

fighting what I assumed was a bad stomach bug. It turned out that I had a perforated appendix. In fact, I was later told that I may have had appendicitis for six months without realising it. My healthy body had been compensating until it finally crashed.

I had never been an overnight patient in hospital before and felt overwhelmed by the whole process of being admitted. My hospital experience was made harder by my failure to recover well from the emergency surgery. I needed a second operation and my recovery was slow after that surgery too.

It was a miserable month in hospital. I didn't cope well emotionally. In hindsight, that's not a surprise given the trauma of the surgery, extended use of morphine, inability to eat, near-constant nausea and lack of sleep. My prolonged hospitalisation also left me with a sense of failure. Failure as a pastor for not coping better (whatever that meant) and failure as a dad for not recovering quicker (even though that wasn't my fault).

Looking back, I can see that I left hospital with depression, but at the time I didn't see myself as depressed. None of the medical professionals involved in my care asked me questions about mental health and I didn't volunteer any information. As far as I was concerned, I was just recovering from an operation and things would soon get better.

When things got worse

I returned to full-time ministry a few months after I was discharged. The church would have been very happy for me to take more recovery time, but ongoing irrational thoughts of failure meant that I hid how I really felt and just got back to work. It didn't take long before my mental health started to decline.

From January 2019, things went quickly downhill and my thoughts were increasingly bleak. I felt like an impostor. I read people's minds as I shook hands with them in the foyer and assumed they secretly knew I was an impostor too. It became harder to concentrate on sermon preparation. I struggled to relax outside of working hours. It was difficult to look forward to anything at all. I wanted to escape. Thoughts of self-harm became a daily reality. These normally involved deliberately crashing the car or stepping in front of traffic.

Even then, I didn't get help. Even when I was spending the song before the sermon telling myself to end my life, I didn't get help. Instead, I became an expert in hiding my symptoms. A mixture of paranoia and pride led me to continue my pastoral duties. If I admitted my problems, wouldn't that just prove I was an impostor? Wouldn't that end really badly?

Getting help

Thankfully, in a moment of clarity one Wednesday, I sat down with Hannah (my wife) and shared everything that had been going on. As a sign of my distorted thinking, I still insisted on leading the prayer meeting that evening! But with her encouragement, I saw a very helpful GP the following day, who prescribed antidepressants and referred me to an occupational therapy team.

That left me with the terrifying question: what about the church? Who could I speak to? What would happen next? I sent an ambiguous text to one of the elders who was a GP. We met that evening, I told him everything I had shared at my doctor's surgery in the morning and he persuaded me that I definitely needed a break. I then spoke individually with the other elders and we agreed an open-ended period of leave with their full support. At this point, the rest of the church wasn't told the nature of my illness; my paranoid mind couldn't cope with more people knowing.

My sick leave ended up lasting five months. Many

of those days were very dark. At my lowest, I made a specific plan to end my life. For weeks, Hannah hid the house keys at night to stop me acting on my plan. But my diagnosis helped me to understand that I was genuinely unwell and gave me some hope that things might get better. Gradually, with the encouragement of friends, the support of therapists, and the grace of God, things did get better.

Some good friends

Looking back at those five months, one of the things for which I am most thankful is God's provision of a number of good friends to support me. Foremost among these was my wife, Hannah. Her own previous experiences of depression made it possible for me to speak openly with her, even about my suicidal thoughts. Some of my experiences must have been difficult for her to process at the time but she was always ready to listen if I needed to chat. She was very good at helping me to notice signs of progress when I wasn't able to see them myself. She also encouraged me to get out of the house for some physical activity. The daily exercise of the morning school run was probably one of the most important aspects of my initial recovery.

There were some other friends who also encouraged me to leave the house. Although the list of people who knew my diagnosis was initially small, there were a few local church leaders I shared with as time went on. They would contact me with invitations for a walk, or an evening of board games, or coffee, or homemade pizza making. It was helpful that they took the initiative with specific invitations because I wouldn't have had the motivation to suggest something if they had just made a vague offer. These friends were always happy to chat about whatever was most helpful – sometimes my health, sometimes a spiritual topic, and sometimes seventeenth-century witch trials (to take a random example).

When I did discuss my mental health with these friends, I was grateful that they didn't pretend to completely understand what I was going through. In the last few years, I have occasionally spoken with people who have compared their own ordinary experiences of low mood with my persistent clinical depression. Although these people have meant well, I confess I have found it difficult to receive their comments in a positive way. But where friends were ready to listen, even if they had limited personal experience or advice, I found this valuable.

As well as these Christian friendships, I made some helpful short-term friendships through the sessions run by my occupational therapists. I attended a five-week group therapy course for people unable to work because of depression and anxiety. The course content itself was highly varied, as it was prepared from a non-biblical 'me-focused' perspective – although I recognise there was helpful material when I talked it through with my wife afterwards. But it was valuable to spend time with people who genuinely understood my experiences and were on a similar journey. We're no longer in contact, but I am thankful for the short time I spent with them.

There were other friends who (understandably) struggled with knowing how to encourage me. In the period when fewer people were aware of my depression, some guessed the most helpful thing was to give me space to recover, unless I got in touch with them. This lack of contact, however, ended up fuelling my paranoia, and I invented irrational reasons why they hadn't said anything since I last spoke to them. I was unlikely to contact people to disprove these irrational thoughts because it was a real struggle to initiate conversations, even by text. It took me three weeks to reply to one voicemail message asking how

I was! Despite my delay in replying, I was actually very thankful for it. Just like the other short messages I received, it was an encouraging expression of concern.

Returning to ministry

I spent a lot of my sick leave assuming that I wouldn't ever be a pastor again. It was difficult to imagine returning to church responsibilities. My memories of ministry were dominated by the final few months of pastoring, with their accompanying paranoia, sense of failure and thoughts of self-harm. But over time, by God's grace, my health improved and my outlook changed. In July 2019, I was able to begin a phased return to my role.

At a human level, my fellow elders played a crucial part in my return to full-time ministry. I had been very aware of their support throughout my sick leave. They placed no pressure on me in terms of recovery, but were happy to keep patiently praying and listening. Some of them knew more details than others, but they all took confidentiality seriously with whatever they knew. Before I returned to work, they wrote to my GP (with my consent) to ask for her opinion on my readiness to resume responsibilities. This was done with a respect for my privacy, not requesting more detail than was strictly necessary. Given my previous premature return to ministry, this was a sensible approach.

As my sick leave ended, I decided to share with our church membership the reality of what had been going on in the previous year. We held a members' meeting where I shared a statement and then another elder spoke and fielded questions. This wasn't an easy thing to do, but I was encouraged by the examples of other pastors who had spoken openly about depression. The meeting went much better than my anxious mind anticipated, with few questions and many expressions of support, and I think the opportunity to share in this way was a mutual blessing.

The following months of phased return involved ongoing conversations with the elders as well as routine GP appointments. During this time, my mind continued to raise questions about my ability to serve in my role but I was now in a better position to manage and challenge these thoughts. In my thinking, I often returned to the description of Jesus in Hebrews 2:11 as the one who is 'not ashamed' to call me a brother. As the Man of Sorrows, Jesus understands the pain and darkness of this world, because He experienced it Himself. He wasn't ashamed of me in my struggles, even with my messy thoughts and antidepressant prescriptions. Instead, He was ready to offer strength and help with real sympathy and kindness.

Ministering out of depression

Another passage that has been helpful to me in my journey with depression is 2 Corinthians 1, especially the reminder that God works through the most hopeless situations in life to make us better able to comfort others. Two years on from my diagnosis, I can see something of how God is continuing to shape me as a pastor and preacher through my depression. Even those weeks where I was able to do very little were not wasted by Him.

At a basic level, my own experience of mental pain has left me better able to sympathise with those facing similar struggles and more aware of what it might look like to be a good friend to those who are depressed. It is, of course, possible to support people with depression without experiencing it yourself, and I still have much to learn, but God works through the circumstances of our lives to enable us to serve others. For me, this includes working through my struggles with depression. Now that I'm in a position where I can speak openly about my own story, I trust that the Lord might help others through my testimony, just as I was helped previously by hearing from others.

I've learned a lot about myself in the last few years as well. Depression is a very humbling experience. This led me to reflect on my own human weaknesses and made me more willing to accept my limitations. Pastoral ministry can be a perfect environment for setting unrealistic expectations for ourselves and others, but the Bible shows us how God's power works through weakness. In 2 Corinthians 1, Paul's trials were a lesson in learning to rely not on himself but on God, who raises the dead. Depression has helped me learn a similar lesson – although I am not learning the lesson as quickly as I might like!

Depression has also forced me to reflect much more on my emotions, which in turn has made me more willing to think and speak about emotions in my ministry. My appreciation of the Psalms has grown a lot in the last few years, and I've become more thankful for the range of human emotions they express. Men are not always encouraged to talk about how they feel, and being a British pastor can add to the temptation to ignore this aspect of our humanity. I think I now have a healthier approach to emotions – even if my own are not always as healthy as I would like. I hope this is reflected in my preaching and pastoral ministry too.

One other character lesson from my mental health journey has been patience. Things have changed so much since my lowest point in early 2019, but it has taken time. It has been a long road of looking to God, with periods of waiting where not much seems to move forward. I'm aware that more waiting may lie ahead too if my situation changes. My family will tell you that I'm still not perfectly patient, but my experiences of depression have given me a more realistic perspective on change and a greater recognition of the fact that God often works at a different pace than we would like.

Keeping going

As I write these words, my journey with depression continues. I still take antidepressants every morning. I have some better weeks; I have some worse weeks. Thoughts of self-harm are now rare but other symptoms continue to be very familiar. At the same time, I am writing this after several months leading a church through a global pandemic. By God's grace, it has been possible for me to keep going in ministry with depression.

An important part of keeping going has been

learning to be open with God about how I am doing. The Psalms give us a liberating example of openness in prayer, including with feelings of despair, fear and abandonment. There is no mental health stigma in heaven and my Father knows I am only human. In my depression, I can sometimes forget this wonderful truth, but talking honestly with God is an ongoing source of strength and encouragement.

Speaking with other people has also been helpful, just as it was in my initial period of recovery. I am thankful for a few friends who I can speak with honestly and remain especially grateful for the continued support of my wife Hannah. As an introvert with depression, I'm not always in the mood for conversation, but when I am, it can help me to process my thoughts and give me a reminder that I'm not as isolated as I might feel. Being able to speak openly with the elders at church means that I know I will be supported if I need more time off. I have occasionally shared something in more general terms, either in a church prayer meeting or the weekly church news email. Short messages of encouragement from church members continue to be a blessing.

In recent months, it's been valuable to have the opportunity to hear from a few other pastors facing similar struggles with depression. I am grateful for these brothers who feel able to speak about their experiences, offering another reminder that I'm not alone, and that it is possible to keep going. Looking back, I think it would have been helpful to hear more about mental health in ministry during my theological training or in a fraternal context. It would be good for this to be a topic that's regularly addressed to guard against pastors entering mental health crises unprepared.

At a practical level, alongside medication, I continue to think about patterns of self-care. For me, a walk after lunch is an important part of my daily routine. I am more alert to the correlation I experience between the tidiness of my study and my mental health and I make sure that time away from my desk is safeguarded. On Sundays, I always have a bath in the early afternoon, with some radio accompaniment to help me relax. If I'm struggling with anxiety, there are things I know I can listen to or watch that will help. I think about all of these things in advance because my depression is not always conducive to spontaneous decision-making and I find familiar routines helpful when things feel overwhelming.

Above all of these things, when I look back at the last few years, it's clear that I'm only where I am by God's grace. When I've felt unable to keep going, he's kept me. That's a comforting thought when I look ahead into the future. I don't know whether my depression will be a life-long struggle; I don't even know what mood I will be in next week. But I do know that the Man of Sorrows will remain with me and, one day, all this darkness will end.

5

Derek's Story

Derek French,
Retired Pastor and Mission Worker

How it all began

Some things creep up on you without you realising what's happening. That's how it was with my depression. It had been building up for much longer than I had ever realised.

The first thing that made me aware something was wrong was that I noticed my sermon preparation was beginning to take longer and longer. I remember hearing one pastor at a conference saying three hours was the maximum one should spend on a sermon. I was shocked by this as by then it was taking me at least eight. This progressively got worse. My difficulty in concentration meant I had to spend more hours studying and this was like a vicious circle. But as I said, it was a gradual thing that happened over a period of many months rather than a sudden jump. As a pastor, preaching was central to my ministry. It was something I knew the Lord had called me to do and I loved doing it, so I kept at it even though my efficiency declined rapidly over those months. I was not at all aware that I was nearing burnout.

I also found my sleep was being disturbed. Normally I can sleep through a thunderstorm but I suddenly found myself fully awake at 2 a.m. and my mind would be racing from one thing to another. None of these thoughts were linked to any crisis in the church, because there weren't any. In fact, the fellowship within the church and encouragements we experienced were reason to be very thankful to the Lord. There was no reason for issues at church to keep me up at night. When I eventually did get back to sleep, it wasn't restful and could be quite broken. The end result was that, when I woke up in the morning, I still felt weary. This, of course, only added to my difficulties with studying, and indeed anything else I did.

The area where we were living was quite demanding. We had many callers at our home. These were people with a great variety of social needs who would call at all hours of the day and night. Our home was attached to the church building and this made it convenient for people in the neighbourhood to see when we were around. These calls would often lead to gospel opportunities, for which I was grateful, but at times they were relentless – at least that's how it felt. It wasn't that these needs were any different to those in other places, but there was such a high concentration of them because so many people lived in the area. We had several hundred windows looking down on our back garden and people used to say we were living in a goldfish bowl. In fact, we found that unless we got in the car and drove away, we could never have a family day together because as soon as we were home people would phone or ring the doorbell. All of this contributed to increased weariness. But I have to say, we were not unhappy with the situation, it was simply very demanding.

At the time, I couldn't see what reasons lay behind my feeling unwell. But I did know that something was not right and I realised I needed help. So, I visited my doctor, who told me she had suffered in a similar way after working in the area for several years. She advised me to take a month off work, which set alarm bells ringing.

The problem was, the next Sunday evening there was to be a baptismal service, which I desperately wanted to take. My GP reluctantly agreed for me to do it, but said I was to see her first thing on the Monday morning after the service.

I got my sermon preparation done and everything was ready for the meetings that Sunday. But I didn't manage to conduct that baptismal service in the end. As I stood to lead the morning meeting, I felt as if an express train had hit me. I suffered a huge panic attack and all my strength seemed to disappear. I had to hold onto the lectern to stop myself from falling over. Surprisingly, no one but my wife was aware anything was wrong. I carried on with the meeting, clutching onto that lectern, but by the end of the service I went home and collapsed on the sofa. I was absolutely exhausted.

I still couldn't understand why this had happened. In my thinking, there was no logical reason for it and I found that very disturbing. It was then that depression took on a new meaning for me and I was eventually diagnosed as suffering from classic anxiety-based depression. At first, I was spared the feeling of deep darkness which is so characteristic of depression, but that feeling of anxiety became my daily companion, and it was made worse because I couldn't think what there was to be anxious about. What might be obvious now was certainly not clear at the time. Alongside all of this was a dreadful feeling of guilt for being so unwell. Concentration also disappeared. Reading anything became very demanding. When I did read something, I could scarcely tell anyone what I'd read. I could just about cope with reading a short passage of Scripture and no more.

Help received then a second dip

My doctor knew exactly what I was going through from her own experience. I found it helpful to have someone who had been where I was. I was put on antidepressant medication and was signed off work for many, many months. I really couldn't do very much at all. Because things didn't get better quickly, I also became an outpatient at the local hospital and found good support there. I took an anxiety management course, which helped me learn how to relax a little. This was useful because I felt under constant stress. The church was also understanding. One of my fellow elders was particularly helpful as he had known similar difficulties in his own family. But it was like being in a tunnel without any light, not even at the end.

Things began to improve very, very slowly. As such, it was decided I should return to work very gradually and to start reducing my medication. Unfortunately, it was not long before I suffered a second dip. The doctors realised that I should have stayed on my medication until I was coping with the return to work, but that had not happened and so I went downhill again. This time, the darkness I referred to earlier became a reality. This made it an especially difficult period.

As this was the second time around, I knew what life was going to be like. This made my depression much worse. Up until then, my Bible reading – I often had to read a passage several times for it to sink in as concentration was difficult – and prayer times with the Lord had been very precious. I could tell Him exactly how I was feeling and knew He was listening. I couldn't pray for any great length of time, but could often pray in short bits. However, this second time round, as the darkness enveloped me, I felt as if the Lord was 1,000 miles away. I knew that He wasn't in reality, as Scripture assured me that He never leaves or forsakes His children, but I felt utterly alone. I did pray, but prayer was so difficult that it felt like my words were just bouncing off the ceiling. I can remember telling myself that my feelings were deceitful and that God never lies, and I clung on to His promises which became my lifeline. I knew the Lord was keeping me by His grace but I didn't always feel He was. I was cast upon Him as never before, which is always a blessing however hard life may be. The darkness of those difficult days made me appreciate in a much deeper way what I had always believed; that to know the Lord was more important than anything or anyone else, and that apart from Him I could do nothing.

Throughout all of this time, to have the loving support of my family – especially my wife – is something for which I am truly grateful. The reality is, it was not only me who was suffering. She and the children were too. In the Lord's mercy, I began to regain strength. Two retired pastors and their wives came alongside me to help share in the preaching and visitation. One couple eventually moved to the area and were a tremendous blessing, both to our family and the church.

Because I was so unwell for such a long time, I have come to accept that I will always have that vulnerability. This is something I have to live with and I need wisdom to pace myself, which is not always easy to do. Before I was ill, my diary was booked with Sunday preaching dates up to four years ahead. After becoming ill, I had to learn to say 'No' and then not to feel guilty about it. This took me a very long time to come round to. Someone kindly bought us an answerphone so that we could have an undisturbed evening in as a family (voicemail was still a thing of the future). But the first night we switched it on, I found it almost impossible not to pick the phone up. These were things that all had to be taken on board and learnt over time. A real blessing to me was having an allotment where I could go and spend an hour or so and do some physical work. This really helped to rest my mind, and I know others have found similar things helpful.

Coping now

I have found that if I overdo things my body tells me very quickly. However, accepting that fact and seeking to live accordingly is something I have to frequently remind myself to do. It is so good to belong to the Lord who is amazingly merciful to His dear children. Communion with Him has become increasingly precious. We may not always understand why certain things happen to us, but He always does. To be able to rest in His sovereign overruling of all things in my life, with the assurance that He even uses those painful times for my good, is a real bedrock on which to rest.

One of the ways the Lord encouraged me during those first tough days was through letters and messages received from other pastors who had been through similar experiences. I had no idea some of these men had grappled with depression until they told me. At least one of them shared with me that he had been unable to preach at all for more than a year because he was so unwell.

It has also been encouraging to have the assurance that other members of the church have been praying for me, as well as believers from further afield. Their love, patience and faithfulness, even when little was said, was a real help to me. I recall one person who simply put his hand on my shoulder and didn't say a word, but he thereby expressed his love and compassion in Christ for me. That meant so much at the time and its memory still stays with me many years later.

Unhelpful things

There were those who wrote or said things that were not too helpful. These things did, on occasion, have some detrimental effects. I am sure that most of these folks thought they were helping, but alas, they did not help at all. Comments such as, 'Pull yourself together', or, 'Get a grip of the situation,' were never going to help and were always more likely to increase my depression. These sorts of comments imply you don't really want to get better, when inside you are crying out that there is nothing you want more. Interestingly, most people who say these sorts of things are never able to tell you where, exactly, you are supposed to 'Pull!' Others very quickly tell you, 'You should not be on medication.' That can be particularly frustrating when the person saying it happened to wear glasses! On the other hand, I remember asking a Christian doctor how long they thought I would need to be on my antidepressants and their answer was so helpful. They simply said, 'As long as the Lord wants you to be on them.' That lifted a huge burden from my shoulders and helped me to be really thankful to God for the medication He had provided.

One thing I found especially difficult in the early days of my illness was when brothers or sisters in Christ asked to know what I was going through. I found that this tended to make me re-live the ordeal and would, more often than not, send me downwards again. I know they did not mean me any harm at all, but had they just thought a little and simply assured me of their love and prayers, that would have been much better. Even now, many years after I was first ill, it is still not the easiest of things at times to share.

Another unhelpful thing is when fellow believers ignore or avoid you. Sometime after I was first ill, I recall being invited to attend a fraternal held for Christians in the workplace of one of our church members. The speaker dealt with depression in a helpful way. In the discussion that followed, I mentioned that I had also suffered in that way. There was an immediate reaction from most of the other believers present and, when the meeting had finished, they nearly all deliberately avoided speaking with me. Were they afraid? Did they think I was from another planet? Were they fearful this was contagious? I really don't know. What I do know is it left me feeling very isolated and discouraged when it should have been otherwise.

Finally, let me address one more unhelpful comment. One person simply told me I was wrong to be depressed! That, as you can imagine, was not helpful at all.

Cheered

Despite the unhelpful comments, there were many others who graciously prayed for me and encouraged me, often in what might seem small and insignificant ways. One church member simply sent me a bookmark with a helpful verse of Scripture on it. Others did nothing more than come to sit with me. Sometimes we talked about the Lord, but we might have just chatted about their family or other things. But they knew that I might not cope with much more than ten or twenty minutes of their time and so they made sure they didn't overstay. They left when they could tell I had had enough. In the very early days, I couldn't cope with anyone calling at all. But the Lord had already given me a loving wife for whom I thank Him so very much. In the early days, the weight of running the home fell on her shoulders as I was simply unable to do very much at all.

Ministry

There is always the danger with depression that you think you are the only one feeling the way you do. But as I've mentioned, the Lord has taught me that many of His servants suffer in similar ways and that has been very helpful. There is also the danger of thinking that the Lord could never use anyone like you again. Such thoughts can be a result of depression itself. It bears saying, I think this is one of the ways the enemy of souls will attack the Lord's servants when they are down. The truth is, the Lord delights to use the weak things of the world, ensuring the glory is entirely His. What a privilege to be in the hands of such a God as ours!

Such experiences inevitably affect one's ministry. I feel, in my case, that it has given a deeper sense of compassion and empathy for others who suffer. Not only for those who suffer with depression, but also those who face other difficulties. The Lord's tender dealings with His servants when they are at their frailest is so instructive. Knowing you have received that care yourself imparts a deeper sensitivity towards others in their trials. Psalm 145:9 tells us that the Lord is good to all and His mercy is over all He has made. That remains true even when our times are very dark indeed. He never lets His children go. Neither does He let anyone snatch them out of His hand (John 10:28–29). These are tremendous realities with which the Father reassures His suffering children and is one of the precious privileges of ministering His Word, in His name, to His people.

6

Dan's Story

Dan James, Assistant Pastor, Avenue Community Church, Leicester

My experience of depression wasn't caused by full-time ministry but it has helped me to think and react differently to others going through depression now. It has also developed in me a desire to identify, love and support people in ministry who are suffering from mental health issues. While a lot of my story relates to a time before I entered full-time ministry, it has shaped my perspective on caring for people battling depression, particularly other ministry workers.

How it started

I was always a fairly happy-go-lucky sort of person. I was probably more confident in myself than my abilities warranted, but nonetheless always keen to be sociable. But shortly after my sixteenth birthday, I found an increased dissatisfaction with life, especially things that I used to enjoy. I also developed an inability to concentrate, sleeplessness and a growing hatred for myself. I don't like using the word hate, but it is the most accurate word in this instance. Whatever I did, I found myself intensely disliking. Even after otherwise enjoyable social times, I would return home and spend sleepless nights going over everything I had said and done, berating myself for it all. I had no way of expressing this self-hatred to anybody and the growing anger I felt towards everything, particularly towards myself, led me to begin self-harming. I would try to keep it secret, cutting my upper arms so they were covered by my clothes but the wounds got deeper and more frequent. I was pretty good at masking what was going on. I would often be the life and soul of a social gathering but all the time my self-loathing grew.

I started to fantasise about dying. Or, more accurately, about not being alive anymore. I could see the Humber Bridge from my bedroom window and the idea of jumping off it filled a lot of my spare time. I tried to keep my thoughts increasingly busy and distracted. I poured my time into music and playing the guitar, but these things only masked the problem.

I would have called myself a Christian when the depression kicked in, but by the time I arrived at university I was in a theological mess. I knew the gospel, I could tell you the five points of Calvinism, I even believed them, but my experience of the Christian life was confused. I didn't find (what I considered to be) joy in my salvation. In fact, I found mostly guilt. I would turn to Psalms 13, 88 and 143 regularly and read myself into them.

I was placed on some medication around this time. Initially, I was given Seroxat, which was considered a 'cure all' for depression. It was hailed as non-addictive, but studies found that not to be the case. It was also found to increase desires for self-harming and this immediately made me wary.[1] As a result, I didn't commit to any long-term medication until I was twenty-four; something I regret in hindsight.

Reckless behaviour

University continued to be a mixed time. My usual cycle of socialising and self-hatred continued, though I now had a few friends who periodically checked in on me, especially in respect to my self-harm and suicidal thoughts.

But I remained unwell. My memory of my second year at university is largely non-existent. It is as though somebody wiped that part of the film of my life. I have flashes of memories from that time, but since then people have often commented on things that I did during that year and it's like I am hearing about them for the first time. My clearest memories are of walking over the Humber Bridge late at night daring myself to jump. I'm thankful I never did.

Sadly, I do remember some of the things I regret the most. I would bounce from girl to girl, throwing myself wholeheartedly at each one in the hope that this might somehow snap me out of the depression. Worse, I would do reckless things that I knew weren't in keeping with someone claiming to be a Christian. I did things that caused a lot of harm, things of which I am deeply ashamed. I am not trying to blame those things on my depression or suggest my depression excuses my behaviour in any way. To be utterly clear, it doesn't. Nor does it let me off the hurt that I caused to others. This is simply to say, a lot of my reckless actions were sinful ways of trying to mask and medicate the emptiness I was feeling. I was looking for a saviour, something to make me feel well, but I was looking to all the wrong things.

I wasn't just reckless with girls. I would spend ridiculous amounts of money (that I clearly couldn't afford) to try and feel better. I would use the majority of my student loan, even my overdraft, on CDs and other unnecessary stuff. On more than one occasion, I found myself unable to pay my rent until the next pay-packet came in. I had this money from my job as a care worker in the local psychiatric hospital. This was the one thing that filled my day and took me out of myself. Spending time caring for others, rather than focussing inwards, helped immeasurably. What is more, earning some money helped with the usual panic caused by my reckless overspending.

I was always fairly bright, so was able to cope with the degree without too much stress. However, by my third year, the pressure of deadlines became unmanageable for me. In particular, the level of concentration required, whilst running on three hours of sleep a night was not sustainable. In the end, I dropped out of university. This only added shame and embarrassment to the cocktail of negativity. To cope, I started to drink regularly.

I spent the next few years trying to mask my real feelings in public. I was now frequently drinking too much, something I had never struggled with previously.

I began to treat women worse than before. Yet my fantasies about death persisted. I was in a dead-end job, having (in my perception) failed at my degree, failed as a Christian and failed financially. I was miserable and didn't want to live anymore.

The majority of this happened when I was younger than twenty-four. But I am convinced of 2 Corinthians 1:4, 'He comforts us in all our affliction, so that we may be able to comfort those who are in any kind of affliction, through the comfort we ourselves receive from God.' That is part of the reason why God allows suffering and affliction. It is so we can use the comfort we receive in those afflictions to comfort others. I am convinced that one reason the Lord led me through all of this is to be of use in my ministry in the future. Ultimately, so I am in a position to comfort others who felt like I did.

The importance of listening

Some of the most unhelpful reactions came from people who would react instead of listen. Sometimes the reaction was one of utter disgust. For example, when I built up the courage to talk about my struggles with self-harm and suicidal thoughts, some people would react with shock and revulsion. They would tell me how those things were sinful and that Christians shouldn't think them. Of course, I already knew that. I already beat myself with that stick plenty. But this reaction almost always shut down any further conversation. The people who helped most were those who would simply listen. They would try and feel the pain I was expressing, rather than condemning the sin I committed (and, let's be clear, it was sinful!). These were people who didn't look disgusted when I talked about the self-harm and self-hatred. These were the people I could talk to about what I was experiencing.

Not everyone's experience of mental illness is identical. Like psychological snowflakes, each is unique. So, it is important not to presume that someone's experience will be the same as ours if we've been through it ourselves. By all means, try and use experience to empathise and suggest things that might help. But we have to realise they won't work for everyone. Lots of people recommended more exercise to me; going for a run or something. Now, at the time, I was physically active – walking a lot and playing for the university basketball team. I would be exercising four or five times a week. But I found that after exercise I would feel worse. I don't know why, but however the chemicals in my head were functioning, the endorphins didn't seem to kick in.

Also, I absolutely hate running. I am not built for long-distance running and really do not enjoy it. I am built for stop-start exercise like basketball or football. So instead of telling me to go for a run, organising a kick-about in the park was much more helpful. Nevertheless, while it can be helpful for many, and I would still recommend exercise if I was counselling someone with depression, we need to recognise it isn't a guaranteed fix. This underscores the importance of listening to the people we're trying to help. Listen to their response to your suggestions as well as what's behind the objections and the barriers. For example, it might be that going for a run enforces feelings of isolation and loneliness, and that the social aspect of different activities would be more beneficial. Listening is desperately important.

The need to challenge sin

If I was telling a fellow Christian about my reckless use of money, or my terrible treatment of women, and they didn't at some point call me out on my sin, it would limit how much I would heed their counsel. Even if they were the best listeners in the world, if they weren't straight with me about what I already knew, how could I trust them to help me with what I didn't know? Even with my reckless living and my personal disregard for holiness, I needed people to call me out on it; people who would force me to face my sin despite my illness.

Though it is important to listen well, we must not be afraid to question how coping mechanisms (excessive drinking, porn usage, extreme consumerism or whatever) square with the life of a professing Christian. Sin needs challenging – it is certainly what I needed. But either I kept my sins hidden from my Christian friends or they didn't feel brave enough to challenge me. The one person who did was a non-Christian friend who called me out on my behaviour. It was the slap across the face I needed. In our desire to be a good, listening ear we must not be afraid to challenge sin.

Similarly, we must ask big questions, even when we are scared of the answer. It is important to ask questions like, 'Have you had any suicidal thoughts?' or, 'Is there any temptation to self-harm?' In asking, there is little chance of planting thoughts in that person's head that they won't have had already. I wouldn't volunteer this information unless directly asked. We need to stop being afraid to ask about these things. In fact, it's more loving to ask the difficult, awkward questions than to not. Questions like that may just save a life. It gives a chance to challenge, lovingly, damaging thought patterns and sins, as well as highlighting the seriousness of the situation.

Pray for and with people

I remember the phone call clearly. It was late at night, and I was very lucky to have a good friend who was awake and chatting to me with whom I could be honest. I expressed my complete inability to pray or read the Bible. So, they calmly said, 'Then I'll do it for you.' It was just like Sam carrying Frodo up the hill in *The Lord of the Rings*, except instead of towards the heart of Mount Doom, it was towards the heart of heaven. They read part of the Bible to me and prayed for me. It wasn't just prayer about me, but placing themselves in my place and praying on my behalf.

When the clouds of depression block our path, it may feel like God is hiding, or that His affections towards us have changed. Despite all our theology telling us that's impossible, we feel otherwise. Instead of freaking out at what sounds like unbelief, meet this person in their worries and their feelings. Psalm 88 is a great example and tells us this is not unbiblical. Stand with this person, read and gently apply the truths of Scripture to them.

While spiritual intercession is important, it isn't the only helpful thing. I remember when I was particularly low, a friend turned up unannounced with some snacks and a film. We didn't talk much, just watched the TV and sat together. Forcing a bit of normal enjoyment into a situation where I wouldn't have pursued it on my own did me good. Those suffering depressive episodes in the ministry would benefit from such things too. Watch TV with them. Take them to the pub. Be normal. Being treated with kid gloves, like a bomb that might go-off at any time, is generally unhelpful. Enabling them get out of their own thoughts can be a great help. Don't underestimate the power of mundane distraction.

Fear of medication

Following on from my early experience with antidepressants, I didn't commit to proper medical treatment for a long time. Occasionally I would go to the doctors and be prescribed something, which I would take for a few weeks or months and then bin. There were several reasons why.

Firstly, some of the antidepressants tended to numb me. That emptiness, the absence of feeling, was – in some ways – worse than the feelings of turmoil. I was lucky that none of the drugs I took gave me physical side-effects but the emotional numbness was horrible. This led me to stop taking them.

But, if I'm honest, another reason was that I was afraid of getting better. I was afraid that, without my depression, I'd be nothing. I was desperately lonely despite being surrounded by people. I craved affection, attention, care and love. I convinced myself that the one part of me that kept those things coming was my depression. People were only interested in a problem to solve or a wound to heal. Who would I be if I didn't have this angst? Boring. Uninteresting. Unlovable. Those thoughts seem embarrassingly pathetic now, but – though I might not have ever voiced them that way at the time – I know that was part of it. My identity was so wrapped up with 'being a depressed person', that losing that part of me would have been like losing a limb. It was like a mental Stockholm syndrome – I both loved and hated the depression. I wanted rid of it, but was terrified of being without it.

Need of the gospel

What is the solution? Being reminded of the truths of the gospel again and again. We need them applied both now and when we are better. Depression skews one's perspective on everything. Medication can, and does, help with that. But only the gospel can show someone what they really need above all. It is the gospel that tells a person they are completely loved, accepted and known by the God who created and designed them for greater intimacy than they desire. This is a God who doesn't see them as merely a depressed person, but as a dearly loved child. Let's not forget the gospel in counselling our depressed friends. They may know it very well. I had been taught it from birth. But I needed it applying afresh by the Holy Spirit, through my friends and church, to see who I really am in Christ. The drugs might work, but the gospel is far more effective and the medicine we all need.

Be patient

However, there is unlikely to be a silver bullet that will entirely cure depression. Certainly, the right drugs can help. But finding them can take months, even years. When I did resolve to get better, it took over a year to find the right medication and for it to take effect. I'm thankful for my wife (then-fiancée) for being patient with me.

But seasons of depression are open-ended. They may pass in a few weeks or months and be relatively mild, what I call 'The Greys' (after a song by the band Frightened Rabbit). Or, they may be longer lasting and more severe. In our quick-fix culture, it can be easy to get impatient as supporting and caring for someone drags on and on.

Patience is key in supporting someone battling depression. They will be feeling impatient themselves, wanting it to be over as quickly as possible. However much of a drain on your time and energy they are, they will feel it is so even more. Patiently love, support and seek to understand their thought processes. I'm very thankful that I haven't had any severe bouts of depression since I've been married, but my wife has. I know how draining, tiring and terrifying it can be to support a spouse through mental illness. So, if the person we're supporting has a spouse, check in on them too.

Depression can take a long time to get over. It can take a great deal of time, effort and energy. There is no guarantee of a cure either. But we still believe God's words to Paul later on in 2 Corinthians: 'My grace is sufficient for you, for my power is perfected in weakness.'

In ministry

My depression did not magically disappear when I started in ministry. One of the key things God taught me throughout my illness was that my feelings don't change God's truth. My feelings and emotions – no matter how dominant and overwhelming – do not change the things that God declares to be true. Having people in my life to remind me of those truths that I couldn't see at the time was – I believe – life saving. Being reminded of God's affection for me as His child, that if God has declared me righteous in Christ then I don't have the authority to declare myself anything else, was vital. I was reminded of God's faithfulness despite my weakness. How I felt about these things did nothing to change the truth.

But it also helped me when discipling and counselling others going through mental health struggles of their own. I am not afraid to ask the difficult questions about suicide and self-harm because I recognise their importance. The conversations on the back of those questions, because of my own experiences, have been much more helpful as a result. I can now watch out for the tell-tale signs of depression – particularly those trying to cover them up – and can be more helpful than had I never gotten ill.

It has helped me care pastorally for people in my church. It has also given me a desire to support other full-time ministry workers who might be struggling.

In the end, my depression remains a constant reminder of my own weakness. To remember how dark things got, how destructive and sinful I had been, is a stark reminder of where I could go again if I am not careful. I know that I need to put certain crash barriers in place going forward to stop my illness developing that way again. Ultimately, when the darkness starts to creep in, I know that I need to tell someone. I have a few people I trust who I can tell when it begins to grow. I've found that if I shine a light on the darkness quickly, it can't grow. That's been an important measure for me to take.

Awareness of my own weakness and temptations has also led me to get formal support and counselling. My wife and I have been under a Christian counsellor with whom I have been able to speak candidly and honestly. This has allowed me to process things more helpfully. I feel fine currently, my depression is barely present, but the suicidal thoughts and feelings I had in the past still lurk in the background. As such, I want to use the means God has provided to keep these things at bay.

7

Jim's Story

Jim Sayers, Pastor,
Grace Church, Didcot

'Preach the word; be ready in season and out of season; correct, rebuke, and encourage with great patience and teaching' (2 Timothy 4:2).

That was my calling! The compulsion of those words had gripped my conscience from my late-teens and propelled me through training into Christian ministry. In 1995 we moved to Suffolk where I became pastor of Kesgrave Baptist Church. 300 people turned up for the induction. It was a special moment. I had found my vocation and gladly put my hand to the plough.

Preaching in the fog

Four years later, halfway through the Sunday morning sermon, I was aware that someone was preaching, but through the mental fog it took a while to realise that it was me! I felt weak, my voice had no energy and my head was swimming. I clung to the lectern, stuck grimly to my notes and nosed through the mist to the final hymn, which I didn't have the energy to sing, before rattling off a benediction. I stepped off the platform and told my church secretary I was heading straight home because I wasn't well.

After my wife Helen had served us a Sunday roast, I refused pudding ('Things must be bad!' she thought) and took our two-year-old upstairs for her nap. She went to sleep quickly, but I remained restless. I sat there wondering what was up. Is there something wrong with my body? Maybe it was my thyroid, or perhaps something worse? What about the evening service?

I turned to a book I had been reading about a church-plant in a nearby town, and went back to the chapter on burnout. The book spoke about the strange dynamics around the church leader, especially if they have been instrumental in helping someone come to faith or were significant in their discipleship. Everybody seems to have an ideal of what a church leader should be. With so many different views, it is impossible for one person to fulfil all expectations. We know that leaders are not superhuman, but because a pastor is a natural focal point, it is so easy to feel important when he or she pays us attention and as though we are missing out if they don't.[1] This author was describing my situation. These were the burdens that had been weighing me down to breaking point. As I read, I found myself sobbing. Helen came into the bedroom to see what the matter was.

'I just can't take the service tonight,' I told her.

'Can't you just pull out an old sermon and get through it?'

'I really can't. There's nothing there.'

I rang the church secretary. He was the voice of sense and compassion.

'Jim, I've seen this coming for a while. Don't worry about tonight's service. You get some rest.'

That evening, he gathered the deacons and they agreed to give me a week off and more time if I needed it. As my responsibilities fell away, an initial sense of relief swept over me. Sleep came easier.

The next morning, I had some energy, so I went to a shop to buy some wood. I had started building a Wendy house for our two girls. Now I could get on with a tangible project that would make me feel good. Halfway round the shop, I felt so faint that I had to lean against a shelf to avoid collapsing. I got home and booked a doctor's appointment.

Growing self-awareness

My GP looked at me knowingly across the desk.

'Do you think you are depressed?' she said.

'I don't think so. I've never suffered with depression. I think it's more likely to be something wrong with my thyroid. Why am I putting on weight?'

She ordered a battery of blood tests and booked me for another appointment a week later. My sleep continued to be disturbed. I would wake early with everything churning in my head. My powers of concentration had gone.

Ministry responsibilities had been taken off me, but I was also involved in work to publish the *Praise!* hymn-book within the year. My section of the book had been demanding my time for a couple of years. Helen agreed I would feel better when the job was done, so I brought the computer home and did a couple of hours each day. Email was still rare in 1999, so I saved each file in three different formats on floppy disk. One error and it all had to be done again. What would usually feel like a joy to me had become a ball and chain. I was also a governor in the local primary school. This was a great opportunity to serve the local community but it also meant more pressure and another big chunk of my time.

Four years into my ministry, there were tensions in the church. A number of people left and I knew, in each case, I was the reason why. There were strains in our youth and children's work and we were grappling with a safeguarding policy for the first time. The church was operating a model of pastor, church secretary and a board of deacons. There had never been an eldership, but the church secretary effectively carried that role with me. Cecil was a wonderful counsellor and friend, without whom I wouldn't have stayed. Even so, the burden of expectation on me as the pastor was huge and I allowed it to consume me.

Helen and I were in our early-thirties with two children under five, so our hands were full and money was tight. Our youngest was waking up bright as a button most nights and one of us had to take her downstairs at 2 a.m. We sat and watched the BBC Learning Zone together, the surreal world of learn-a-language programmes, and she sat on my lap and laughed at me as I fell in and out of sleep.

The effect of sleep deprivation on both body and mind is immense. We are a psychosomatic whole of body and soul. If the body is exhausted, it affects the mind and the nervous system. On the one hand, we may show neurological signs. The night before my last foggy sermon, we had been at an evening wedding reception. Normally we would love to ceilidh together, but one dance was enough for me. My head felt like it was wearing a lead helmet. I sat out the rest of the evening, disorientated by the noise.

On the other hand, our senses are dulled so that we do not react to pleasure, encouragement or good news. Our motor reflexes may not be so quick, and coordination may falter. We become less aware of our low moods, and blame everyone else. I vividly remember coming home for dinner one weekday, and within ten minutes I had managed to upset Helen and both daughters so that we were all in tears.

Back at the surgery, the GP looked at me with a knowing expression:

'I'm glad to tell you that your thyroxin levels are normal. All your blood tests have come back clear.'

Then came the hammer blow.

'I think you need to admit you are depressed. I am going to sign you off work for a month, and we will see in a month's time if you need longer. I am also going to prescribe you a low dose of dothiepin.'

I can still remember walking from the surgery to the Tesco pharmacy, half wondering whether to bin the prescription and walk home. My better side said, 'At least get the tablets and then decide.' I am so glad that I did. I took one at bedtime and a weird thing happened. As the drug took effect, the tangled thoughts, fears and worries of my mind closed down one by one. I slept better than I had in weeks.

A diagnosis of depression came as a shock to Helen as well as me. We both had to process it and talk as a couple. How would this affect our future? What role did Helen have to play in my recovery? The answer was – a huge part! While I was signed off work, we could take some time to be together, free from the ministry stresses that weighed on both of us. We could also make some plans together to make family life more sustainable in the future.

A slow recovery

Medication did not return me instantly to normality. Together with being signed off work, it gave me the space to work many things through at a deeper level. It was important in those early days of recovery to get sleep. It might be two hours in the afternoon, which would leave me awake at night, but the advice from the GP was, 'When your body says "sleep", don't resist it.'

As I clicked 'Save' on the last file for the *Praise!* hymnbook, other areas of life began to clear as well. It was obvious that I had over-committed. Someone told me to buy an answerphone so that 5–7.30 p.m. could be proper family time. As well as Saturday being my day off, I agreed I would stop feeling guilty about taking Monday morning off too when I returned to work. Channel 4 had just launched a new programme – *Grand Designs* – which captured my imagination and I began dreaming of my own self-build. Finishing the Wendy house was the closest I ever came to realising it! But that taught me something about my besetting sin of escapism. It is good to have hobbies that take our mind off work, especially if they are something tangible like woodwork. But I would rather dream of another world out there and it can always be more fascinating than the job in hand. When life in front of you is depressing, your mind says 'Go on! Imagine that timber self-build in rural France. You deserve it! Where's the harm?' But that sows the seeds of discontent and the devil piles in to depress you further with everything that is wrong with your church, marriage and whole life situation. The green-eyed monster doesn't cause depression, but he does feed on a fertile imagination that isn't currently enjoying much about life.

The greater realisation as I recovered was how low my spiritual life had become. Standing by the sea in Felixstowe and watching the ships come and go is fascinating. Some are piled high with containers, their vast hulls riding low in the water while a grain ship might sail up the Orwell to fetch its load, riding high with lots of the hull above the water line. In our walk with the Lord, what burdens do we carry ourselves? When we try to carry them in our own strength, we are like the cargo ship riding low in the water, going twice as slow because so much extra burden has to cut through the waters of life. In Christian ministry we should rejoice that we have good news to share, but if the wonder of God's glory and the richness of His grace is not feeding our own souls, that can be a profound cause of depression. Often, if we have unresolved guilt in our soul, it will eventually show in physical stress on the body (Psalm 32:3–4). If we take God for granted, and try to press on in ministry in our own strength, he has a way of hiding his face until we cry out for him (Psalm 30:6–12).

On the other hand, physical exhaustion can be the cause of spiritual depression. When facing trouble in Asia, Paul felt he was 'completely overwhelmed— beyond our strength' that he reached the stage where he 'despaired of life itself' (2 Corinthians 1:8). Physical exhaustion led to this spiritual challenge. The spiritual can have physical effects whilst the physical may have a spiritual impact. My heart and soul had been so taken up with the tasks of Christian ministry that my passion for Christ had faded. I simply hadn't noticed. Had I really worshipped God rightly when leading others in worship? Now I had to watch others lead worship and think about how I approached God.

We went away for a weekend to Helen's parents and I wasn't much company as I recall. On the Sunday afternoon, I felt the urge to drive to Oxford and go to the evening service at St Ebbe's Church. Most of the students had gone home for the summer so there was plenty of room to find a seat. Alone before God, I quietened my heart in his presence. Vaughan Roberts began a summer series that evening on Christ in the Old Testament, preaching on Deuteronomy 18:15: 'The LORD your God will raise up for you a prophet like me from among your own brothers. You must listen to him.' He linked it to the baptism and transfiguration of Jesus, two events in the gospels that glimpse the glory of Jesus before the cross and resurrection. The surety that Christ is indeed the fulfilment of all that Moses and the prophets have told us, that he is the glorious Son of God, and that we must listen to him, poured joy and relief into my soul for the first time in some while. A sense of the true glory and authority of Christ broke through into my soul. Why had my focus not been upon him? Why had serving Jesus in the task of ministry turned me away from him? That evening was a turning point in my recovery.

Returning to work

I returned to work after a two-month break, having agreed with the GP that I should double my antidepressant dosage. We didn't have a Holiday Bible Club that August and I set the bar low in what I aimed to do. Some folk were very supportive, several were wary of being too eager to discuss depression and someone referred to my illness as, 'This thing you've had.' Those that knew all about depression from their own experience opened up and were very honest and supportive.

However, I wasn't ready for what came next. The tensions in the youth and children's work had pent up over the summer and things boiled over in the autumn. The danger with depression is that you handle problems alone, and badly. Depression can mean a low, suppressed mood, or it can push us to the upper end of our emotions in destructive ways. Put that together with a model of church leadership where the pastor is the only elder and you have a recipe for disaster. I failed to control my anger at what was going on and I completely mishandled the situation. Several people left the church and others were wounded. It seemed to usher in a period where the church felt becalmed for a long stretch.

Looking back, I can see God's hand keeping us going. A dentist and his wife, the kind of people who radiate Christian hope and good cheer, came into the church from London. What they made of us after being in a big city-centre church I really can't imagine, but they both ladled out encouragement, love and prayerfulness in all directions. They were only with us for a year, but what good they did! Another couple came who would be essential in growing the youth group. God knows who and what we need and when we need it. He is so gracious!

That November, I went away to the Proclamation Trust Minister's Conference. Those conferences sustained me through some tough times. I had come near to the end of my bottle of tablets but forgot to get the prescription renewed before I went, not realising until it was too late. I decided to take one tablet a day, instead of my usual two, to get me to Friday. I remember getting up one morning and opening a newspaper. The Queen had awarded the George Cross to the RUC as part of the Northern Ireland peace process. Over 300 RUC officers had been shot dead over the years, and they printed a photo of each one of them; 300 faces staring at the camera, all suddenly taken into eternity. I can be fairly hard-hearted with the news, but I found myself crying. I needed those tablets more than I knew. The dark of November was not the time to come off them and it was stupid to try without the GP's advice. With her help, the following spring I reduced the dose until our Easter holiday, when I was finally off medication for good.

Outgrowing the ingrown church

The local high school made regular visits to our church to find out what Baptists believe. We would open the baptistry so that 150 Year 7 pupils could walk in one side and out the other. Each time we took the lid off, I wondered how long it would be before we actually needed to fill it for a baptism. I started to read Jack Miller's book *Outgrowing the Ingrown Church*. I took it away on holiday that Easter. That wonderful book changed my life. It proved the spiritual turning point both for me and for the church.

A church becomes 'ingrown' when it is taken up with meeting and operating as usual. Nobody expects anyone to be saved. There is no hunger for the Spirit to move in a powerful way. There is tunnel vision about how the church operates; things that failed in the past put a brake on trying anything new. A sense of having most things right pervades church life, rather than a hunger to grow in grace and a passion to reach the lost. Criticism is damped down, though there is plenty of gossip about others, as people seek to justify themselves. The pastor and his wife work within an unexpressed social contract:

It states that the congregation will support, honor and pay the pastor and his wife as long as they are inspiring yet dignified, sweet but saltless. In return, the pastor, assisted by his spouse, is expected to do all the real work of the local church—that is, he is expected to do his own work and everyone else's too. The net effect is that he moves at an exhausting pace that leaves no time for witnessing, solid study of the Scriptures, prayer, and the meditation that builds faith filled with the fire of God's presence.[2]

This describes what I had been doing and why our church felt stuck.

Miller goes on to explain how a church needs to become gripped with a sense of the glory of God and that we are a royal priesthood (1 Peter 2:9) who serve God joyfully and proclaim Christ earnestly in our communities. The book led me to read more widely, and to explore the website of Jack Miller's mission agency, which was then World Harvest Mission, where their emphasis on sonship was worked out in more detail. The missing doctrine in our church was adoption. As Christians, we are adopted into God's family and can call him Father. We are justified by faith in Christ alone and so we have nothing to prove. We participate in the divine nature (2 Peter 1:3–4). Yet we often live as spiritual orphans, serving him joylessly as slaves, with no sense of intimacy with him or any dependence on the power of his grace in our lives. No wonder church life gets stuck in a rut. We need the renewing power of the Holy Spirit to refresh and strengthen us.

I came back to church that summer and preached a series on sonship as all the key ideas tumbled out of Scripture into my heart. As I tried to apply them to our church life together, our prayers were quickened, people sometimes ended the service in tears at God's Word and we began to see people of all ages come to faith. Our young people's group began to thrive and within two years we had baptised six people. Most of all, I had learnt the lesson that I need to learn again and again: it is only in Christ, and depending totally upon his grace, that we can be of any use to him in ministry. When we find Christ to be our joy, our 'refuge in each deep distress', our 'strength and glorious righteousness', then we can walk (or maybe, like Jacob, limp) through the valleys of life, with their chasing shadows, and find in those times that our ministry is the richest and most blessed that we will ever know.

Depression doesn't go away. Encountering it full-on in 1999 made me realise that I had probably lived through other bouts during my student days that I hadn't understood at the time. It is now a normal facet of my life, something to be lived with, that means I must be more self-aware and take care. Every April I seem to have an episode following the Easter break. I have no idea why it should be then. On sabbatical in 2007, I started a blog as a way for the church to keep in touch with what I was doing. In one post, I described the depressed mood I had been through that April. The elders and deacons (we had appointed elders by then) said I must take that post down as it would deter anyone from sharing their pastoral needs with me. They were insistent, so I complied. That was a while ago and, more recently, I reposted it because I think it is important to be honest about depression. Depression doesn't just hit me once a year. I need to be continually aware of it, and I know the black dog stalks many people much more closely. It really is okay to admit to not being okay, even for pastors. When we admit it, people will open up to us with their own pressures and burdens and we may find we can be more help to them as a fellow-sufferer than they ever expected. We might also find that they also help pastor us, as they should!

Conclusion

Stephen Kneale

If you have now read through the different stories of pastors who have struggled with depression, you won't fail to have noticed the common themes. There will always be some common features for anybody experiencing depression. For example, as noted in the introduction, to get a diagnosis of depression you must have at least five out of nine DSM-IV symptoms. Inevitably, then, any two people with depression will have at least some symptoms in common. But there were also some significant differences too. What was helpful to some did not help others and what exacerbated problems in one case was not necessarily the same in another.

When we get to the end of a series of chapters like these, it can often be difficult to know exactly what to do with them. We might recognise that pastors get depression, but the variety in the stories makes it hard to know how to help. Which story, for example, most closely resembles what I – or my minister – happen to be going through right now? Here, then, it seems helpful to collate what has been said. What were the things common to everybody, what was significant in several cases and what differed across the whole range?

Consistent for most

In almost every story, there were at least six things that were fairly constant. It is important that we take note of these points because – if our seven chapters are representative – these are the things that will most likely be at issue in other cases. Whilst it is not absolutely guaranteed these things will be at play, they are more likely to be an issue than not.

First, and perhaps most significantly, every story recognised the importance of medication. In all except one of the stories, antidepressants were a vital part of recovery. Even in Alistair's story, where medication was not involved in his recovery, he noted that he always

126

encourages people to seek medical help – including antidepressants – because this is typically important in getting better.

Given how common and vital this was in almost every story, if you are supporting a minister who is suffering from depression, the best thing you can do is to encourage them to seek medical help. Getting the right medication will either resolve the depressive issues themselves or will help get them to a point where they can engage with other therapies that might lead to recovery. By encouraging your pastor to seek medical help, you will be giving them a clear signal they do not need to feel guilt or shame. It will help remove some of the stigma around their illness by recognising that their depression is not primarily a spiritual matter but one that requires the help of medically trained doctors. If you are a pastor experiencing depressive symptoms yourself, if you are longing to be free of your illness, one of the most important steps you can take is to go and see your GP.

Second, almost everybody mentioned how acts of thoughtfulness were especially helpful. Some were unable to take visitors, but knowing that people were praying – without prying or foisting themselves upon the sufferer – was always encouraging. Others spoke of small gifts or notes that were left for them. Others were grateful for specific, rather than general, offers of help and suggestions of things to do with somebody else that might prove distracting. There were examples of people just sitting with folks or watching TV with them. Knowing that people had thought about the situation and were trying to do what was helpful, without adding to the issues, was always well received.

Third, most stories pointed to how talking in some form – usually for limited periods of time – tended to help. Most said that visits from people in their churches were well received. However, a number of stories noted that staying for long periods of time was almost always too much. In some cases, talking therapies such as CBT or other forms of counselling proved helpful. But almost everybody acknowledged the value of short visits. They were enough to give some encouragement and show a level of care and concern. As one story noted – and was certainly true in my case – there will be times when any sort of visit will feel overwhelming. If your pastor is open to visitation at all, 'short and sweet' would almost certainly serve him better. Ten minutes of chewing the fat will do them much more good than overstaying your welcome.

Fourth, there was a significant amount of agreement on the kind of questions that almost always made matters worse. Most noted questions like, 'How are you feeling?' and 'What can I do to help?' were unhelpful. Everybody recognised that people mean well when they say these things, but they are almost always best avoided. The former question suggests a weariness at the length of the illness, while the latter creates another thing to think about and, if they cannot think of a suitable answer, often leads to increased feelings of guilt. By contrast, several stories noted that they were helped much more by people who offered specific support when they didn't have the motivation to come up with ideas themselves.

Fifth, problems were consistently caused by people insisting they knew how the sufferer was feeling or imposing their own experiences onto them. As has been noted a number of times, depression manifests in a variety of ways and what serves one person will not necessarily help another. This is apparent enough simply by reading these stories on their own terms. As such, it is hardly surprising that treating people as though your experience must be the same as theirs is not likely to help. Instead, it is far better to simply allow the other person to share their experience, offering yours where appropriate, and let the one in the midst of depression note any similarities for themselves, such as there are any. Likewise, telling people that we know how they feel has a similar effect. Assuming that we know how someone else feels always runs the risk of misjudgement. Almost everybody noted how unhelpful they found this.

Finally, a number of people spoke of how they found concentration difficult. Some spoke of how hard it was to read the Bible for themselves or to maintain attention long enough to pray even short prayers. At the same time, a number of stories mentioned how helpful it was when Scripture was read and applied to them. Notwithstanding the point above regarding outstaying our welcome, reading the Scriptures when people can't do so themselves and praying with them can be helpful. Several spoke of the importance of remembering what God – rather than their errant feelings – thought about them was especially valuable. In one story, CBT only started to help when it was rooted in an objective understanding of God's view of His children rather than in the subjective feelings of the depressed person themselves. A number of others, whilst not related to formal therapy, relayed something similar. As such, spending short periods of time reading the Bible and praying with someone in the midst of depression – helping them to engage with the Lord's view of them rather than their own feelings about themselves – is likely to be helpful.

The case for several

There were a handful of things that cropped up in several, but not all, stories. Part of the reason for this is that some of these things are context specific. At the same time, as we have noted, people respond to their illness differently. Not everyone experiences the same symptoms, and so the things that are helpful or otherwise, will be impacted by exactly what the person is experiencing. There are also issues of personality at play too. Extroverts and introverts will differ in what they find most helpful and what they perceive they need whilst suffering. Likewise, our own personal sinful tendencies may well affect what we are tempted to do in response to our illness. Some were inclined to look for ways to numb their pain – or find means of feeling anything at all – whilst others looked to different things. Some close down while others become reckless. All of these things will affect personal responses to depression and make a difference to how it is experienced.

A number of stories noted that distraction was helpful. The specific form it took varied – going to an allotment, working on a farm, making flat-pack furniture and watching low-grade TV were all cited as examples – but distracting the person from their own thoughts was helpful for a number of people. It should be said – as in my case – sometimes depression is so severe that attempts at distraction can be counterproductive. It is unhelpful to have people suggest going out for a little walk as a magic bullet when I had, only a day before, tried to take my own life! Distraction is recognised by medical professionals as a useful technique – and clearly in a number of cases it did work – but we must be careful that we don't overplay it. Just as paracetamol can be helpful when we have a headache, it is obviously not an appropriate remedy for somebody who has just broken their arm. That is to say, distraction may well be helpful for the person you are supporting, but it is not always going to fix the problem.

Several stories spoke about the value of being open with their churches, and particularly their elders, when depression struck. In most cases, there was some fear of reaction and worry about what admitting to this illness would say about them as a minister. However, in the stories that noted it as helpful, the church leadership were largely supportive. Of course, we have to accept that not all churches will be helpful. It was noted that the way pastors speak about issues of depression are not always helpful and, in the comments some received from church members, clearly others can be similarly obtuse. Equally, just as there are good and bad people in every job, so there are elders who can be particularly unhelpful when it comes to these issues. Whilst we cannot pretend that openness with our churches will always prove helpful nor that our elders will always be supportive, a number expressed that being so in their case certainly was. Given the consistency with which church leaders were helpful, and the wider point that everybody found talking on some level to be a help, encouraging sufferers to be open with their church leaders seems a measure worth taking. Whilst it is not risk free and by no means guaranteed to lead to care and support, enough found that it did as to make it a likely useful thing to do.

A number of stories highlighted the providence of God in the midst of their suffering. Some were able to point to specific examples of how their depression prepared them for ministry in the future or the Lord had clearly organised events for their good. Others simply referenced God's sovereignty in a more general sense, as a point of comfort to them in the midst of their depression. Nevertheless, although we may not see how God is using depression in any given case, it can be helpful to remind people of God's sovereignty. If there are specific circumstances that we can see unfolding and it is clear how the Lord is bringing good out of the situation (just as He did in Joseph's case in Genesis), pointing people to these things can bring hope. If we cannot see what the Lord is doing at the time – like in Job's case – reminding the sufferer of God's sovereignty and His promises to work even this for their good isn't trite, but ultimately comforting for a believer who already recognises that truth but may not be feeling it in the moment.

In terms of areas in which we need to tread carefully, several things seemed common. A number of pastors spoke of their love for preaching, particular services they were keen to take or a more general desire to press on with ministry. We may look at that as excellent and laudable, but these are key things to watch. Many have a strong work ethic coupled to a significant sense of duty often driven on by more guilt than we care to admit (it has been said, scratch a good Protestant and you'll often find a Catholic underneath). In several cases, this drive and desire tipped people over into a depressive episode. If you are beginning to see these symptoms in yourself or your pastor, be sure to give them permission to stand down and find others who are able to bear some of the load. Keeping a watch on these things could be the difference between averting a serious episode and inducing one.

In a similar way, a number of stories commented on the tendency to put on a mask in church. This is something of which a lot of us – even those who don't suffer from depressive tendencies – are all too aware. Whilst not all will be doing this – some pastors are much more open with their congregations than others – it pays to ensure that we check regularly on how our pastor is doing. Asking difficult questions about appropriate work patterns, proper rest and meaningful family time are all important. But pressing further into deeper heart questions such as what is driving us in ministry, whether we feel we can say 'No' to things and how far we are beginning to feel the ministry depends entirely upon us – aside from having theological implications – may well help us discern the state of our pastor's mental health too.

There was also a recognition that depression can lead us into sinful behaviour. Whilst we want to be sensitive to the fact that an illness may ultimately be driving those sinful decisions, the need to challenge such patterns of behaviour is important. Of course, we are all prone to sin and pastors are by no means exempt. We know, only too well, of ministers who disgraced themselves and brought dishonour to Christ through their sin and none of this was the product of any mental illness. Let's not pretend that doesn't happen with troubling frequency. But there are times when sinful patterns of behaviour might be a signal of underlying mental health issues. Noting this is not to say that such sin should be ignored or given a free pass. It is simply to say – depending on the specific behaviour – it may affect how we approach the issue. For a minister who has suddenly started to drink more excessively, or who appears to be grasping for other escapist means, it is worth asking why such escapism has become more frequent. Could it be that searching for comfort or escape in things other than Christ, sinful as that is, might be driven by more than a mere underlying dissatisfaction but a response to a depressive episode?

In at least two stories, context-specific living arrangements led to a feeling of being constantly watched. Many will recognise, in a less literal sense, that feeling persists among church pastors in general. Whilst the literal windows looking into gardens and church members living across the road fuelled a sense of paranoia or inability to escape, those same feelings are common in the pastorate. The weight of expectation mentioned in at least one story speaks to this issue. Given how widespread this feeling is among pastors more broadly, we must be careful that we manage the expectations on our church leaders and ensure that they (and their families) do not have to deal with the church as though Big Brother is always watching. Respecting the privacy of the pastor and finding ways that he and his family are not always on show would help, especially if depression has taken hold. Whilst we may not always be in any position to decide otherwise, manses immediately next door to the church are not always the gift that we think they are!

Points of difference

Whilst many of the details were different in each case, there are several important ways in which most of the stories differed. Whilst I won't high-light every difference here – recognising that different contexts and situations are rarely going to be identical – there are perhaps four key ways in which these stories differed from case to case.

First, it seems worth stressing that not everybody had suicidal ideation. Depression did not inevitably lead to attempts on life, self-harm or even plans to do such things in every, or even most, cases. Of course, in some cases it did and, frankly, the degree to which it happened varied. Some merely had fleeting thoughts of such things, others made plans whilst others still went much further and tried – several times – to carry those plans out. The point is that depression does not necessarily equate to suicidal ideation. Without getting into all the whys and wherefores, there are circumstances in which suicide is not caused by depression and, likewise, where a lack of suicidal ideation is not evidencing that depression is absent. We must be careful not to assume that the severity of self-harm and suicidal ideation on their own are the only – or even primary – evidences of depression.

Second, we have noted the way in which sinful patterns of behaviour can be intertwined with depression. Minimally, depression has been described as a 'selfish illness' in that it has a tendency to make the sufferer very self-centred. Life suddenly revolves around my personal feelings, function and assumed worth. Very often, the needs of a supportive spouse do not even get a backseat, so much as hog-tied and placed in the boot! But, as already noted, it can manifest in a number of different sinful tendencies.

However, in one story in particular, it was emphasised how important it was to challenge those sinful patterns of behaviour. In other cases, however, such challenge may feel as though one is being blamed for their depressive illness as the patterns of behaviour and medical issues are so closely related. Given the divergence in these things, we need to tread very carefully when it comes to challenging sinful patterns of behaviour in the depressed person. That is categorically not to say that we merely overlook such things and ignore them. It is, however, to say that the manner in which such things are addressed is important and we must take real care to know whether this is a person who requires a straight challenge or someone who needs careful handling to see the sin-issues that may be present.

Third, some described depression as 'coming out of the blue' whilst others could look at patterns and see how their depression had been forming over some time. Where our pastor appears to crash, very often this is the product of pressure that has been building over time, which they may not have noticed themselves. We shouldn't assume that a growing sense of depression in our pastor over time is any less serious than a case that seems to happen more immediately.

Finally, there was a range of things that were considered helpful in each case. Some found things such as exercise and distraction to be helpful while others found they either didn't help or made matters worse. Whilst there is nothing wrong with asking if somebody has tried something that was helpful for you in your experience, it is better when we explicitly recognise that just because it worked for us doesn't mean it will do in this case. Similarly, we need to be careful not to be too prescriptive when making suggestions as to what might help somebody in their depression. As you can see from these stories, not everything helped everybody and what helped in one case didn't always help another. Given the consistency with which listening was advocated, we would do well to listen when people tell us what they have found helpful and tailor our suggestions accordingly.

What do we do now?

Most of us simply want to help our struggling pastor in the midst of any depressive illness they might be facing. We hope that the things written here might give you some insight into what they may be feeling, things to avoid that might make matters worse and some practical ways in which we can genuinely help. Even when we don't do what is most helpful, the majority of pastors recognise – as was stated repeatedly in these stories – that most people meant well and just wanted to help. We should allow that thought to spur us to try and do something rather than let fear of getting things wrong stop us doing anything at all. But, better yet, when we do something, we can now take note of the things written here and try to do what is more likely to be helpful than not.

In the end, however poor and misguided our efforts, we have a sovereign God. All of us are capable of praying to Him and asking Him to comfort those who are afflicted by depression. We also know that, one day, Jesus will come again to make all things new, wiping every tear from every depressed eye. We can all remind our pastor of this truth; the same truth in which they shepherd the churches Christ has given to their care. We don't have to understand depression, in all its complexities, to be able to help our pastor as he suffers with it.

Notes

Introduction

1. S. McManus, et al., *Mental Health and Wellbeing in England* (NHS Digital, 2016), p. 8.
2. Accessed at https://www.mentalhealth.org.uk/news/nine-month-study-reveals-pandemics-worsening-emotional-impacts-uk-adults
3. LifeWay Research, 'Study of Acute Mental Illness and Christian Faith' (2014), p. 5.
4. Accessed at www.nhs.uk/conditions/clinical-depression
5. NICE Clinical Guideline, 'Depression in Adults', 28 October 2009, p. 48.

Chapter 6

1. Sarah Boseley, 'Antidepressant linked to suicide risk in adults', *Guardian*, 13 May 2006.

Chapter 7

1. Diana Archer, *Who'd Plant a Church?* (Christina Press, 1998), pp. 103–4.
2. C. John Miller, *Outgrowing the Ingrown Church* (Zondervan, 1986), p. 35.